Downtown Church

INNOVATORS IN MINISTRY

"Some books might offer a map for a particular type of ministry; not so Downtown Church. This book is more like having a personal tour guide. It speaks with an authority and a vulnerability that come from years of solid experience. Edington guides us into the twenty-first century with a new paradigm for ministry that is Christ-centered, relationally-grounded, and purpose-driven. This book may save some of our most cherished mainline churches."

—Dr. Randy Rowland is author of *Get A Life* and a contributor to Lyle E. Schaller's *Center City Churches*. He is pastor of Church at the Center, a downtown Presbyterian Church in Seattle, Washington.

Downtown Church *will surely be intimidating to the fainthearted. But for those who have the love of Christ and of the people, along with audacity, imagination, energy, and capacity for the hard work needed to be a vital church in the urban downtown, it will be an inspiring challenge to emulate.*

—James O. Gilliam is the author of *Walking on Water*, and former pastor of Plymouth Congregational United Church of Christ in Des Moines, Iowa.

"If you love the city, continue to have hope for the congregation, are convinced that innovative leaders make a difference, and believe firmly in the power of God's spirit, then the chances are that you will read Downtown Church *in a single sitting, as did I."*

—Andrew J. White, Hagen Professor of Practical Theology, The Lutheran Theological Seminary at Philadelphia.

"This book is more than a 'how-to' book. It is a highly personal walk with Howard Edington as he faces the challenges and heartbreaks of a central city ministry. Each chapter is filled with practical insights and revelations of how a pastor confronts both personal tragedy and ministerial success.

—Roger O. Douglas is the rector at Saint Philips In The Hills Parish in Tuscon, Arizona.

In 1961, Lewis Mumford wrote: "Before modern man can gain control over the forces that now threaten his very existence, he must resume possession of himself." That is a spiritual battle, and fifteen years later we have not been successful. In an urban society, that victory must be won in the city. I suggest that you read Pastor Howard Edington's powerful book,—Downtown Church, *and take heart—and emulate it, if you agree.*

—Robert G. Borgwardt was the senior pastor of Bethel Lutheran Church in Madison, Wisconsin from 1963–1991.

Downtown Church

Church

The Heart of the City

Howard Edington
with Lyle E. Schaller

INNOVATORS IN MINISTRY

ABINGDON PRESS
Nashville

THE DOWNTOWN CHURCH:
THE HEART OF THE CITY

This book is printed on recycled, acid-free paper.

Library of Congress Cataloging-in-Publication Data

Edington, Howard, 1952-
    Downtown church : the heart of the city / Howard Edington with Lyle E.
Schaller.
        p. cm.—(Innovators in ministry)
    Includes bibliographical references (p.   ).
    ISBN 0-687-05440-0 (plk. : alk. paper)
    1. City churches. I. Schaller, Lyle E. II. Title. III. Series.
BV637.E35   1996
250.91732—dc20   96-19390
                                                                          CIP

Scripture quotations unless otherwise labeled are from the New Revised Standard
Version Bible, Copyright © 1989 by the Division of Christian Education of the
National Council of the Churches of Christ in the USA. Used by permission.

Scripture quotations noted RSV are from the Revised Standard Version of the Bible,
copyright 1946, 1952, 1971, by the Division of Christian Education of the National
Council of Churches of Christ in the USA. Used by permission.

Scripture quotations noted KJV are from the King James Version of the Bible.

The news articles "New Life, Faithfulness Downtown" and "Edington Ads Whet
New Spiritual Appetite" are taken from *The Orlando Sentinel*, December 16, 1990.
Used by permission.

Excerpts from *FaithQuakes,* by Leonard Sweet are copyright © 1994 by Abingdon
Press. Used by permission.

96 97 98 99 00 01 02 03 04 05—10 9 8 7 6 5 4 3 2 1

MANUFACTURED IN THE UNITED STATES OF AMERICA

In Memoriam
John David Edington
October 8, 1972—December 21, 1994
"A young man forever in the kingdom of God."

CHURCH STREET

PLAY GROUND

KITCHEN

SERVING

FELLOWSHIP HALL

EDUCATIONAL FACILITY & ADMINISTRATION

LOBBY & VISITOR'S CENTER

MAGNOLIA AVENUE

CHAPEL

PLAY GROUND

SANCTUARY

ROSALAND AVENUE

LIFE CENTER

TOWER

MEMORIAL GARDEN

AREA WAY

JACKSON STREET

CONTENTS

FOREWORD

Recently a forty-two-year-old pastor came to see me. He was beginning his third month as the new senior minister of a historic downtown First Church. Back in the 1950s it was identified as one of the most influential congregations in the entire denomination. Two of the most famous preachers of the twentieth century had served consecutively as the senior minister. Sunday morning worship attendance averaged well over one thousand. By the middle of the turbulent 1960s, worship attendance had dropped to an average of 850. The year previous to my visit with this new senior minister, worship attendance averaged 275.

The current picture included these nine characteristics: (1) an aging and shrinking membership, (2) an annual operating deficit of nearly $100,000, (3) a modest endowment fund, (4) a superb location with great visibility, (5) an aging and expensive-to-maintain building, (6) limited off-street parking, (7) a powerful past orientation, (8) several extremely capable "young" leaders in their fifties, and (9) an absence of a distinctive identity in the larger community.

While this new senior minister and I had never met, I knew him by reputation. He was reputed to be an excellent preacher, a venturesome and risk-taking personality, and a creative leader. Toward the end of our two-hour conversation, he asked me what I thought should be the top priorities on his time and energy during the next several months. Many years earlier I had been involved with that congregation in a brief parish consultation and had kept up-to-date through conversations with members and through the grapevine.

In response to his questions I first equivocated by explaining that I was short on recent firsthand knowledge about that congregation and, therefore, he should not give too much weight to my advice.

When he pressed me for specific suggestions, I suggested these might be the top eight priorities on his time and energy:

1. Do not neglect sermon preparation.

2. Earn the trust, respect, and confidence of your leaders.

3. Build a program staff based on a combination of (a) competence, (b) compatibility with your vision for the future, (c) creativity, (d) productivity, and (e) unreserved loyalty to you.

4. Choose a half dozen of your best leaders today and tomorrow and accompany them on two-day visits to three or four outstanding congregations of your denomination that are now modeling a how-to-do church in the twenty-first century.

5. Schedule a series of two- to four-hour meetings with five to seven of your most creative, future-oriented, deeply committed, influential, widely respected, reflective, venturesome, and supportive leaders. Ideally the majority will be persons born after World War II who do not carry any memories of "the good old days here." The purpose of these gatherings is to define a new role for this historic congregation for a new century.

6. With the active support of these and other leaders, communicate that new role to the members and win as much support for it as quickly as possible.

7. Balance the budget by increasing receipts.

8. Celebrate every victory, large or small, during the next couple of years.

In response to his question on this subject, I added that building a big, strong youth ministry probably should rank no higher than seventeenth on his list of priorities.

A few days after that visit, the mail brought the next-to-final draft of the manuscript of this book. If it had arrived a week earlier, I could have given better advice in fewer words: "Take this manuscript to the print shop down the street, copy every page, return the original to me, go home, read it, and adapt Dr. Edington's suggestions to your situation."

This book is the story of a how-to-do church in a downtown setting in the twenty-first century. The origins of this book go back many years to when I was asked to participate in an event for senior ministers of larger congregations to be held in Orlando. As a result of earlier work with several congregations in Orlando, I suggested the schedule include two hours with the senior minister and the program staff at First Presbyterian Church. We all left that experience somewhere between awed and intimidated by the unified support for a common and clearly defined vision for that congregation that was articulated by those eight staff members.

As the years passed, I attempted to continue to be informed about what was happening in downtown Orlando. Thus, when the editors at Abingdon raised the possibility of a series of books on Innovators in Ministry, I immediately decided this was a story that needed to be shared with a larger audience.

When I approached Howard about this possibility, he responded with doubts, hesitation, and an excessive degree of modesty. Thanks, however, to Trisha, Pam, Jim, and Ben, my side won that battle and two years later, we now have that book.

The National Context

What does the future hold for the downtown church?

A widely shared view in the day of the big, strong, vital, influential, mission-minded, and predominantly Anglo downtown congregation, with the tall steeple, ended with the passing of the 1950s. The suburbanization of the Anglo population, the erosion of inherited institutional loyalties, the decline of public transportation, the lack of interest by younger generations in Sunday evening worship, the deterioration of the public school system in dozens of large central cities, the growing expectation that a convenient off-street parking space should be available at the end of every automobile journey, the migration of the big department stores from downtown to the suburban shopping malls, the growing fear of crime, the decline of the Sunday school, the emergence of literally hundreds of very large suburban regional churches, the growing preference by younger generations for the electronic keyboard over the pipe organ, the attraction of television for people's discretionary time, the long commute to work, the migration of most of the high paying jobs from the central cities to the suburbs and the growing shortage of ministers, who are both outstanding preachers and effective leaders have combined to undermine the historic role of scores of downtown churches.

That persuasive argument can be documented by looking at what were identified as the great downtown churches of the 1950s. Most can be placed in one of eight categories: (1) they have relocated out of the central business district to a larger site with more off-street parking; (2) they have merged into another shrinking congregation; (3) thanks to a large endowment fund, they are still viable, despite a shrinking and aging membership; (4) they have dissolved and no longer exist; (5) they are now largely an African American or immigrant congregation; (6) they have redefined their primary role as a social service agency; (7) thanks to a continuing financial subsidy from denominational headquarters, they are able to maintain a modest presence in the downtown community, or (8) they did almost everything right, but their future was undermined by either (a) one tragic mismatch between pastor and parishioners, or (b) a series of relatively brief pastorates of three to ten years each.

Those eight categories account for most of the "great" Anglo downtown churches of the 1950s. Only a fraction are large, strong, vital, future-minded, and exciting congregations that today are able to attract new generations of church-goers.

Where Are the Best Lessons?

While much can be learned from an examination of fail-ures and the explanations for these failures, far more can be learned from successful experiences. While they are outnum-bered by those downtown congregations that have con-cluded their best days are behind them, the first place to look for useful clues to a bright future is in today's strongest downtown churches. A second place to look is at the ministry of the healthiest of today's megachurches, regardless of lo-cation. A third place is those congregations that once were large, strong, vital churches, went through a period of sub-stantial numerical decline, and have come back to enjoy an era of vitality, relevance, and effective outreach.[1] A fourth resource of useful insights is simply to reflect on what to-day's churchgoers expect from the church.[2]

A fifth place to look for wisdom is in those congregations founded as neighborhood churches that have transformed themselves into regional churches. Some of these once were rural churches in a rural community but today are ex-urban congregations serving new generations of urbanites who want to combine country living with a city paycheck. Many more were founded in the 1920s or the 1950s as neighbor-hood parishes on the outskirts of the central city, but the automobile wiped out that role. Rather than attempt to per-petuate the past, they have accepted a new role as a regional church.

The Top Three Lessons

The number one lesson that can be derived from an examination of these five categories of large contemporary Anglo congregations requires use of a word that is ideologically anathema to many of the church leaders born before 1955. One reason for detesting that word is that it stands in opposition to a concept that was the preferred ideological motivation from 1882 through the early 1970s. That old rallying cry was *interchurch cooperation*.[3] The new reality is best described by what many still identify as a dirty word. That new reality is intercongregational competition.

For approximately 350 years of American church history, competition among Christian churches for new members was not widely perceived to be a significant factor on the North American ecclesiastical scene. The distinctive local identity of a congregation usually reflected a combination of at least four or five of these eight variables: (1) the nationality and language of the members, (2) the geographical location of the meeting place, (3) the social class and/or race of the members, (4) kinship ties, (5) inherited denominational loyalties, (6) the theological stance of that congregation, (7) the fact that an hour's journey covered only two or three miles and, thus, geographical proximity was a crucial factor in the creation of social networks, and (8) in many, but not all cases, the person and personality of a pastor who served that congregation for two or three or more decades.[4]

The primary source of identity in the large contemporary Anglo church is in what it does in ministry. Relevance, credibility, and quality have become the criteria for evaluating the ministry of the large Anglo congregation of today. All across North America those three words summarize the criteria used by younger generations as they look for a new church home. Those three words also provide a useful context for understanding the first three lessons to be learned from the large churches of today in general and from the effective downtown churches in particular. What is that number one lesson?

1. Today's downtown church must be competitive.

The three criteria for determining which congregations are competitive in this competition to reach new generations of people are relevance, credibility, and quality. This book is the story of a downtown church that has earned an A on all of those criteria!

The basic generalization on credibility consists of two parts. First, the larger the congregation and/or the younger the new members and/or the larger the geographical area from which the people come and/or the larger the proportion of newcomers who were not reared in that particular religious tradition and/or the higher the expectations projected of people and/or the greater the visibility of that congregation in the general community and/or the more extensive the ministry, the greater the need for credibility. Few people challenge the credibility of the tiny and well-concealed church that specializes in care of the members.

Second, the larger the congregation, the greater the degree of anonymity among the members, and the greater the visibility of that church in the larger community, the more likely that the number one source of credibility will be, not in the denominational affiliation, but rather in the person of the senior minister. That is one reason why the sacred journey of this senior minister comes early in this book.

2. Today's downtown church must display a clear identity.

Whether that location in the central business district is an asset or a liability will be determined by the definition of identity and role. In Orlando, one neighboring church of the First Presbyterian Church concluded that relocation to a much larger site and the construction of new facilities was necessary to fulfill its role. That was a wise decision, and the First Baptist Church of Orlando is a model of a creative, challenging, and successful relocation effort to a 120-acre site five miles to the east at a total cost of nearly $40 million. The leaders at First Presbyterian Church agreed on a different role, and that produced the need for a different strategy. This book also is the story of how one downtown church defined a new identity for itself around the slogan, "We're Here For Life!"

The specific content of that identity and role are less important than the fact that it is distinctive, is clearly defined, enjoys a broad base of support, and serves as the guiding light for all policy decisions.[5]

3. Today's downtown church needs effective pastoral leadership. This is not a new idea!

Nearly a quarter of a century ago, Ezra Earl Jones and Robert L. Wilson wrote what became the classic book on the downtown church. In describing what they identified as "A Winning Combination," they identified the pastor as the number one variable.[6]

The pastor, or senior minister, is the key leader in making that church competitive on the current ecclesiastical playing field. The pastor is the key leader in defining identity and role. For many people these variables of relevance, credibility, and quality are a reflection of the person and personality of that long tenured senior minister.

It is important for the senior minister of the downtown church to be a visionary, creative, and future-oriented leader. Even more important, however, is the ability to win the support of followers. Too often personal popularity is perceived as equivalent to followership and when the crucial decisions are made, those visionary plans are lost because of the absence of followers.[7] Fans may not become followers!

A Dozen Other Lessons

These first three lessons from the experiences of high quality and large contemporary congregations are ranked in this observer's perception of importance. Some will argue that leadership should be placed first and my response is, "It's a free country."

This next list resists efforts to rank in order of importance. In one situation staffing would top the list, while in another, preaching would head the list. When the focus is restricted to the downtown church, it becomes even more difficult to rank them, but since I still think sequentially, here is my list:

1. The downtown church offers challenging Bible-centered and relevant preaching. The specific definitions of those terms vary greatly. In most downtown churches, the senior minister is both the messenger and the message. In a growing number, two or three preachers share the pulpit responsibilities every weekend. The only safe generalization is that the combination of relevant messages and superior communication top this list. That explains why preaching deserves a full chapter in this book.

2. The downtown church has a seven-day-a-week schedule. The big difference between 1957, when the majority of people coming to the downtown church came on Sunday, and 1997 can be summarized in three numbers: 24-7-365. That is how the First Presbyterian Church of Orlando describes its schedule—*24 hours a day, 7 days a week, and 365 days a year.*

One reason for placing this so high is that it is the only way to respond effectively to a large range of needs. Another reason is the weekday program is becoming the number one entry point, as contrasted to Sunday morning in the 1950s, for newcomers to the large church.[8]

3. The downtown church needs an exceptionally competent and compatible staff team! For some congregations this is the number one priority for creating tomorrow. This need explains why I first placed this congregation on my list of great downtown churches and, also, why an entire chapter in this book is devoted to this subject. It also is important to add that the two critical words in that statement are "team" and "compatible."

4. The downtown church serves a regional constituency but concentrates on local outreach ministries. In terms of membership, the contemporary downtown church draws members from within a fifteen-to-forty mile radius, but most of the specialized outreach ministries are with people in the heart of the central city. Many of these specialized ministries are delivered at First Church. Most serve a local constituency, but others meet a worldwide need. The after-school program at First Church, Orlando, illustrates a response to a local need. The computer ministry with missionaries illustrates a worldwide outreach. A growing number of downtown churches are launching a variety of off-campus ministries with people who would never come to that big intimidating building. [9]

5. The laity are trusted in the downtown church! A persuasive argument could be made that the biggest change in American Christianity since the 1950s is an expansion of the role of the laity. Two of the foundations for this change are trust and training. It is no coincidence that three of the Christian bodies in the United States displaying the largest decrease in membership operate on a polity based on distrust of the laity. One of the central themes of this book is the influential role of the laity.

6. Prayer is a central component of the life of the downtown church. American Protestants have rediscovered the power of intercessory prayer and that, also, is a continuing thread in this book.

7. The downtown church understands that relationships have replaced role as the guiding principle of life. The references to the death of John David Edington, the responses of the people of Orlando to that tragedy, and the sermon that concludes this book underline that theme.

8. The downtown church is sensitive and responsive to the needs of people. Back in the 1950s, society allowed most churches to operate on a producer's agenda. Most churches offered two choices: "This is our program and schedule. Take

it or leave it." That day disappeared with the close of the decade called the 1960s. One definition of relevance is, "That speaks to my needs." New generations bring new needs and new agendas. Sensitivity to those needs is a key to ministry in the twenty-first century.[10]

This, incidentally, is why life in the downtown church is increasingly complex and also explains why the demand for competence keeps rising. A willingness to try is no longer an adequate substitute for skill.

9. The downtown church places a premium on the teaching ministries. This is placed this low not to reflect a minor importance because it ranks far higher, but because effectiveness requires a competent staff, an unreserved trust in the laity, relevant training experiences, a recognition of the power of intercessory prayer, an understanding of the implications of relationships replacing role, and an affirmation that the teaching ministries reach far beyond the current membership.

10. The downtown church recognizes the power of television. For many downtown churches, television is the most productive single channel of communication for inviting people to come to church. In the very large markets, costs currently limit the use of television, but the technology of the twenty-first century will eliminate that barrier. Television may be more influential than real estate or staff in reinforcing identity and explaining role.

11. The downtown church cannot be afraid to ask people for money! A fair number of readers will move this up to number two or three on their list of the variables that distinguish the effective large church of today. Dr. Howard Edington describes how he asked people for money in Orlando. The reluctance or the inability to ask people for money is the number one self-limiting factor in thousands of churches today.

For a growing number of downtown churches, many of the dollars will come to separately incorporated 501(c)3 single purpose agencies designed for a specific ministry. Most or all of their receipts come from corporations, foundations, nonmembers, and governmental agencies. Thus far, African American churches have been more effective than the predominantly Anglo congregations in utilizing this system for financing new ministries.

12. The downtown church should expect to become an influential player in the decision-making processes of the community. A strong argument could be made that the one distinctive characteristic that sets the First Presbyterian Church of Orlando apart from nearly all other predominantly Anglo downtown churches is that it has earned the right to be a player. That is a role that must be earned. It is not awarded as a prize! Once again, African American churches have been more effective than predominantly Anglo congregations in earning a voice at the policy-making tables.

While many readers may differ over the ranking or wording of these fifteen lessons, they do provide a context for reading this case history of a remarkable downtown church. More important, these lessons and this inspiring case study can be useful for leaders in other downtown churches who believe God is calling their congregations to a new role in a new century.

Lyle E. Schaller
Naperville, Illinois

PREFACE

INTROSPECTION:
My Sacred Journey

I was at Granddaddy's home at 1305 Dauphin Street, Mobile, Alabama. The house was a large two story frame house (white, of course, with deep green shutters, a long veranda and massive columns), nestled in among the safe protective arms of two magnificent oak trees, both ages old. In summer the rooms of that house were always cool and fresh as the ceiling fans click-clicked, click-clicked, and in the winter they were warm with the delicious smells of logs burning in fireplaces framed with ornately carved mantelpieces.

Entering the house by the long front hallway, I would pass the stairway leading up to the second floor, pass the tall hand-cranked Victrola whose tinny speaker spun out to me the likes of "Peter and the Wolf" and "Barnacle Bill the Sailor." I would glance in at the formal living room on the left, a room filled with antique furniture and fascinating treasures, my favorite being a large gold clock with a spinning pendulum, an *eternity clock* (time and eternity all rolled up into one). The clock was encased in a huge glass dome. I never see that wondrous object in my mind's eye that I do not also hear with my mind's ear, "Look, but don't touch."

Straight ahead was the dining room with a table so long that four nuclear families could cluster about it as an extended family every holiday. Oh, how comfortable and protected we were in those great explosions of love and joy and food and unforgettable memories!

But for me, all of these rooms served only as a passageway to the library, Granddaddy's favorite room and mine as well. It smelled of old books, heavy wood paneling, and the faintly lingering aroma of Granddaddy's smoking tobacco. He had suddenly stopped smoking a year before, and at the time I did not know why. Shelves lined the walls, and books lined the shelves: law books (he was a judge), history books (he could recount events from ancient history as if he had been there), and books of sermons and theology (his faith was towering and he regularly took to the pulpit as a lay preacher).

That night—I was thirteen years old at the time—at his invitation, I joined him in the library, sitting with him in his favorite chair. I had done that so many times when I was younger. I could still fit because he had got so small, as if he were shrinking while I was growing. I listened eagerly as he began to read to me. I can still see the book in his hands. Its cover was dark, something between deep red and maroon, and the front was etched with the outline of a great ocean-liner. What he read to me that night was the story of another night, a night in mid-April of 1912, when the *Titanic*, the greatest ship ever built up to that time, went down in the icy seas of the North Atlantic, her hull having been ripped wide open by an iceberg. The ship that people believed could never sink, slipped quietly, almost gently, beneath the waves, carrying some fifteen hundred persons to a watery grave two miles deep in the cold and silent sea. I remember the words Granddaddy then read:

People have never been sure of anything since. The unending sequence of disillusion that has followed cannot be blamed upon the *Titanic*, but she was the first jar. Before the *Titanic* all was quiet; afterward all was tumult. That is why to anyone living at the time, the *Titanic* disaster, more than any other single event, marked the end of the old days and the beginning of a new, uneasy era.

Now, years later, I know book and author by name: *A Night to Remember*, by Walter Lord. Granddaddy put down the book and reached over to pick up his Bible from its permanent resting place on the table by the chair. He said, "Now son, I want to read to you a story about another night and another sinking boat." He turned to Matthew 14:22-27 and read to me these words:

Immediately he made the disciples get into the boat and go on ahead to the other side, while he dismissed the crowds. And after he had dismissed the crowds, he went up the mountain by himself to pray. When evening came, he was there alone, but by this time the boat, battered by the waves, was far from the land, for the wind was against them. And early in the morning he came walking toward them on the sea. But when the disciples saw him walking on the sea, they were terrified, saying, "It is a ghost!" And they cried out in fear. But immediately Jesus spoke to them and said, "Take heart, it is I; do not be afraid."

He did not read the whole story. He stopped precisely where I just stopped—"But immediately Jesus spoke to them saying, 'Take heart, it is I; do not be afraid.' " Then Granddaddy put his arm about my shoulder and said, "Son, you are growing up in an uncertain, uneasy world. But I want you to know that there is something we can be sure of. I want you to remember that when nothing else seems certain, Jesus is. Other things may change or disappear; Jesus never will."

That is all he said, or that is all I remember of what he said. But those words burrowed down into my young heart like seeds planted in spring in a plowed, fertile delta field. Other seeds had been sown earlier by the Spirit of God. Still other seeds would be sown later by that same Spirit. It took a long time for those seeds to grow, but grow they did. The day came when I offered myself for the gospel ministry, believing that I was called to preach "something we can be sure of."

In retrospect, taking that significant step was inevitable given the circumstances. Jesus said once, "Unless you change and become like children, you will never enter the kingdom of heaven" (Matt. 18:3). In other words, he was calling us to a childlike trust and faith. While I can take no credit for it at all, my life has been marked by those qualities. I grew up in a home where the air that I breathed was filled with the faith and where I was surrounded constantly by the powerful, palpable presence of Jesus Christ. In my growing up years no part of my life was apart from Christ.

As a child I spent a lot of time in and around the church. I loved the church, everything about it, everything in it, everything associated with it. For four generations members of my family have been engaged in the Presbyterian ministry full-time. (My daughters, Meg and Beth, mark the fifth generation.) Furthermore, those members of my family not in the ministry have been lay leaders in the church, absorbed in their commitment to Christ and devoted to the work of his church. I am especially proud of the witness of my mom and dad. He preached every Sunday and she sang in the choir. That meant that every Sunday my two younger brothers, Will and Van, and I were left to sit near the front without benefit of parental supervision. That landed us in trouble on more than one occasion, until the time (and just recalling it provokes a measure of pain) when my father stopped his sermon right in the middle, pointed his finger at us in the pew, corrected us from the pulpit, and then right there in front of God and everybody else ordered Will to move up one pew. Immediately my father picked up his sermon at precisely where he had so suddenly stopped. I can tell you that from that point on we were most attentive!

Through it all I loved what I heard and I loved what I saw. Many times in my childhood my dad would go to preach in little rural churches on Sunday afternoons. At one point he was responsible for a circuit of seven small churches in south Alabama, and I would go along to keep him company. It was there more than anywhere else that I began to see the transforming impact that the preaching of God's Word can have on the lives of people. I came to love preaching—and I came to love preachers. Many times great preachers of that day would come to preach in my father's church and they would stay in our home. While spending time with them I sensed their spiritual power, was warmed by their radiant joy, and was inspired by the reality of the Christ I saw at the center of their lives. It was in the midst of that kind of family and that kind of atmosphere that I grew up. Consequently Christ, and the thoughts of Christ, and the things of Christ came to me as naturally as eating and breathing.

Sometimes I have found myself envious of those who have had a dramatic conversion experience to which they can point and from which they can draw a powerful testimony. Only the wisdom of the years has caused me to see that that envy is misplaced. I have come to realize that God uses dramatic, even supernatural means, to call people to himself only when those individuals are far removed from Christ and the Kingdom. Paul needed the cataclysmic experience on the Damascus road because it was the only way God could capture the attention of one so antithetical to the Kingdom. I needed no such conversion experience because I never knew anything but Christ in my life. Besides, I would never exchange for anything in the world my childhood experience of growing up in such a loving and faithful family.

However, when I was a senior in college, God did orchestrate a wondrous event in my life that proved to be pivotal for me. I fell in love with a beautiful blonde, blue-eyed girl. Eventually Trisha would become my wife, but first she became an instrument in God's hands to inject new life into my journey with the Lord. She had a great faith of her own and she kept prodding me with questions about my own faith. It was out of that experience that I came to realize the faith I had cherished as a child had become layered over by a veneer of selfish desire and pseudosophistication. She encouraged me to strip away the veneer and embrace the Christ. I did, and I found myself confronted with my unmistakable call to the gospel ministry. That sense of call has undergone an occasional "course correction" over the years; sometimes it has even wavered, but it has never died. In fact, there is greater urgency to it now than ever before.

The journey in the ministry has taken me and my family to three pastorates before Orlando: the First Presbyterian Church of Kilgore, Texas; Shandon Presbyterian Church in Columbia, South Carolina; and the First Presbyterian Church of Pine Bluff, Arkansas. While in each pastorate it was my intent to stay for the rest of my life, and while each had its own inherent value, I now realize that God meant for those three pastorates to be his fine-tuning mechanism to prepare me for the complex, sometimes overwhelming, demands of the downtown church.

Frankly, I confronted the challenge in Orlando with the same mixture of fear and uncertainty that gripped the disciples in that small boat on the Sea of Galilee. The storm blew up high and unrelenting. Fear and despair terrorized them. But just at that point, the Bible, with its exquisite economy of words, says Jesus, "came walking toward them on the sea." Then Jesus, who could calm any fear, calmed theirs with the words, "Take heart, it is I; do not be afraid." He was all the certainty they needed and he was all the certainty I needed as well.

Under the direction of God's Spirit, I claimed the three great lessons God had taught me in my earlier pastorates and I applied them immediately and directly to the ministry in Orlando. Those three lessons I regard as worth sharing:

Lesson One: Put Christ First—For the past twenty-five years I have carried in my wallet a letter from Margaret Dodson, my mother-in-law. Early in my ministry she heard a sermon I preached and in response she wrote these words:

I thought your sermon was well thought out and beautifully phrased. However, I feel like the woman who pressed a paper into her minister's hand one Sunday. On it was written, "Sir, we would see Jesus." Only the church has the unique message of Jesus Christ, Son of God, Savior of all, who can transform people's hearts and change the world. Paul and Peter took every opportunity to preach that message. Now the opportunity is yours. Howard, through you we would see Jesus.

I carry that letter to remind me to always, but always, put Christ first.

That lesson was reinforced by those three remarkable congregations that I served prior to Orlando. I learned that when you put Christ first, people are moved to share their faith, an evangelistic fervor takes hold, and the church begins to grow. I learned that when you put Christ first, people develop caring hearts and compassionate spirits and give themselves sacrificially to meeting human need in whatever form it appears. I learned that when you put Christ first, racial barriers come tumbling down like Jericho's walls after the trumpets, social demarcations are obliterated like sand castles by the incoming tide, economic differences are ground away like boulders under the ceaseless pressure of a glacier, and, as a result, people, who otherwise have nothing in common, discover the uncommon commonality that is theirs in Christ. It does not take a rocket scientist to see the value of such a lesson for the work of the downtown church.

Lesson Two: "Stir What You Got!"—My uncle, Dr. Andrew Edington, long time college president and noted teacher of the Bible, is a character in the colloquial sense of the word. Sunday evenings he travels from his home in Kerrville, Texas, to the Texas State Prison in Huntsville to teach the Bible to the inmates on death row in the maximum security wing. Late one Sunday night as he was returning home, he stopped at a roadside diner in a Texas hill country town to snag a quick cup of coffee. As is typical of all the Edington males, he quickly used all the sugar packets the waitress had left on the table for him, but wanted more. As the waitress came near his table again, he called out, "I want some more sugar, please." The crusty old gal defiantly put her hands on her hips, leaned over toward him and snapped, "Stir what you got!"

That lesson has proved invaluable over the years. No church is perfect, and sometimes you encounter circumstances that make them less than what you hoped. For example, the First Presbyterian Church of Kilgore had oil wells on the property, and the church had thrived for years on the royalty income. Wouldn't you know, I arrived the same month as the *last* royalty check. What to do? Stir what you got! I moved to the Shandon Church in Columbia, a church in desperate need of more property for parking and expansion. Can you believe it? The man who owned the property adjacent to the church had been irritated years earlier by the church bells and had sworn then that the church would never get his property. What to do? Stir what you got! I went to Pine Bluff and six weeks later a tragic airplane crash claimed the lives of Mr. and Mrs. Harvey McGeorge, two of the strongest leaders and most powerful influences in that church. Their deaths created an enormous vacuum. What to do? Stir what you got! In a downtown church with its unique limitations, obstacles, and hazards, this is a lesson I needed to learn. What to do? Stir what you got!

Lesson Three: Don't Settle for Less than Your Best—The first Session meeting over which I presided in Kilgore, Texas, took place between Sunday school and worship. I was more than a little harried and frantic. I had taken off my suit coat but had not yet donned my preaching robe. Suddenly I was confronted by the elders streaming into my office for the meeting. I conducted the meeting in my shirtsleeves. After the meeting, LeRoy Rader, one of the truly great men in Christ whom I have known in my life, pulled me aside and said, "Son, don't ever conduct a Session meeting again without your coat and tie. The people of Christ deserve your very best all the time." Believe me, I have never repeated that mistake.

Excellence is the subject of that lesson. Notice I did not use the word *success*. I used the word *excellence*. Catch the difference? Success means being *the* best; excellence means being *your* best. Success means being better than everyone else. Excellence means being better today than you were yesterday and striving tomorrow to be better than you were today. Success encourages expediency and compromise, prompting us to love things and use people. Excellence cultivates principles and consistency, prompting us to use things and love people. Excellence does not mean being *the* best; it means being *your* best. Therefore, a key element in building a strong downtown church is the pursuit of excellence—excellence both in the church's life and in the preacher's life. Don't settle for less than your best!

Granddaddy was right when he told me that things will change or disappear. Four years later he was dead after a long, lingering, losing battle with cancer. The family, now spread from Texas to Florida to North Carolina to New England, no longer manages to be in one place at one time. That great old house at 1305 Dauphin Street is gone; just a vacant overgrown lot there to mark the place where so many memories were born. Even those stately oaks long since gave way to the stormy blasts of Hurricane Camille. Yes, Granddaddy said, "Things will change or disappear, but Jesus never will. When nothing else seems certain, Jesus is." For fourteen years of leading the great First Presbyterian Church in downtown Orlando, I have lived by Granddaddy's words.

I shall die by them as well.

ACKNOWLEDGMENTS

I get by with a lot of help from my friends! Here are some of them who deserve a special thanks for the help they have given:

My family:

My wife Trisha; my daughters, Meg and Beth, and their husbands, Bill Sefton and Bobby Hewitt—for helping me to remember that while our family has been broken by death, our love for one another remains whole, and one day the family will be whole again in heaven.

My father, David Edington, and my uncle Andrew Edington—for their life-long influence over my earthly journey.

My administrative staff:

Bill Alexander, David Baker, Rob Bullock, Jim Cook, Bill Duckworth, Gordon Hatcher, Beth Edington Hewitt, Kerry Jones, Ben McKenney, David Patrick, Ted Pierce, Roy Riviere, Donna Speer, Kent Sterchi, and John Tolson—for sharing this ministry, stoking the fires of my spirit, and standing firm for Jesus Christ in the heart of this city.

My partners in this project:

Ann Brown, Rob Bullock, Bill Peterson, and Pam Theall—for applying their considerable skills and technical expertise that transformed the thoughts of my mind into words on the page.

My friends along the way:

John Rife, Don Brown, Ruth Carter, Ron Harrison, and Carolyn Wine—for their willingness to be used by God to call me to this church.

LeRoy Rader, Heyward McDonald, and Steve Matthews—whose call to previous pastorates helped prepare me for this one.

Bob Buford, Fred Smith Jr., and Robert Schuller—for inviting me to speak at conferences where this book found its genesis.

David McKechnie, Louis Zbinden, and John Stevens—significant ministers in their own right who encouraged me to share the story of my ministry.

Libby and Clarence Laird, Betty and Tom Mobley, Pat and John Lile, and Mildred Everett—for the gift of friendship and unceasing encouragement across all the years of my service to my Lord.

The members of my congregation:

For allowing me the privilege of being both their minister and their friend, with special thanks to those who have shared their thoughts and let me tell their stories.

My mentor:

Lyle Schaller, I thank God for you!

INTRODUCTION

April 18, 1995. My usual morning routine: walk the dog, get a cup of coffee, sit down in my favorite chair to read *The Orlando Sentinel*. This particular morning what I read, however, was anything but the usual. The paper's editorial column featured the following:

New Life, faithfulness downtown

"We were born to unite with our fellowmen, and to join in community with the human race."
—**Cicero, circa 50 B.C.**

About a decade ago, parishioners at the First Presbyterian Church of Orlando wondered if it might not be financially expedient to move the church from the urbanized confines of downtown Orlando to a more suburban setting.

The church's 4.3-acre campus, which now encompasses an entire city block, would have been worth a small fortune, particularly during the real estate boom of the early 1980s.

Instead of cashing in, though, church members opted to stay put, and they refocused their energies on giving back to the very community they had drawn upon for the better part of the past century.

Today those efforts will bear their first fruit as the church officially opens the Clayton Life Center, the first part of a four-phase, $21 milion expansion of community-oriented facilities on church grounds.

The Clayton Life Center, named in honor of the Clayton family that financed most of the construction, is a three-story hub of activity that will offer medical services for the indigent, an Alzheimer's respite center, day care, a gymnasium and fitness center, a library, a computer center, game tables and classrooms.

When the reconstruction project is finished, in about 5 years, the church will have a new sanctuary, fellowship hall, visitors center and educational building—all of which, like the Clayton Life Center, will be open to both parishioners and the public.

The church's pastor, Dr. J. Howard Edington, says the new project is a "mission station" rooted in the 5,000-member congregation's desire, in some conceivable, tangible way, to improve the quality of life in the inner city.

The parishioners of First Presbyterian Church should be applauded for their vision, compassion and generosity to the community at large.

It's projects like the Clayton Life Center that give children a constructive place to go after school, the homeless a place to find medical care, the despairing a place to regroup, and just plain ordinary people a new place to explore.

Way back in 1982, who could have imagined that such words would be written about the First Presbyterian Church of Orlando?

It was in June of 1982 that my ministry at this old, established, downtown church began. And it began against the prevailing wisdom of the day: mainline, downtown churches could not thrive, perhaps could not even survive. A newspaper article presaged the plight of the downtown church in the seventies and eighties.

From a larger context the religion editor of the *Wisconsin State Journal* wrote a provocative article on November 16, 1969, headlined, "Downtown Churches, Victims of a Trend." The writer pointed out that downtown churches throughout the country were in serious trouble. The changing demographics of the inner city, the flight of people to the suburbs, and the growth of strong suburban churches were cited as major factors in the assault on Old First Church.[1]

Furthermore, people whom I loved and trusted, and who knew me and my gifts and abilities, questioned the wisdom of tackling such a challenge. One of them wrote to me, "Howard, the day of the downtown church is over. It is an endangered species, soon to be as extinct as the dinosaur. I would hate to see you take such a dead-end step in your ministry."

Close examination of the facts surrounding First Presbyterian Church of Orlando (hereafter referred to as First Church) at that time underscored the message. Other churches in Orlando's downtown area were either moving to more promising locations, slipping in their effectiveness, or changing their ministry profile altogether. First Church, caught in that same cycle of diminishing numbers and reduced impact, was facing, at best, an uncertain future.

These were the circumstances under which we arrived at First Church in June of 1982, drawn there—no, change that—**forced** there by the Spirit of God. Up to that point, Florida had been a great place to visit, but it was the last place on God's green earth I ever believed I could fulfill my calling. Guilty of typical "stereotypical thinking," I assumed that all the people in Florida were retirees or tourists, and I did not see how a church could be built on either. The icing on this cake I was creating in my own mind came when we, as a family, were considering the move and my nine-year-old son, John David, plaintively pointed out, "But, Dad, where will we ever go on vacation if we move there?" Bottom line? We had no desire to be in Orlando, and certainly I had no desire to be downtown.

When we visited Orlando and discovered that the church had been in a downward slide over a period of years, I wondered why in the world I had wasted my time and the Lord's. But the Lord had a better idea. The Lord, in fact, forced me to accept the call to Orlando. It proved to be, as the Lord's directions always are, an incredible gift. Over the years some amazing things have happened. That old, established downtown church not only survived, it thrives.

In 1982, there were 2300 members on the rolls, slightly more than half of them active. Today the church's membership approaches 5000, with approximately 400 new people joining the church each year. That is just one indicator of the new vision, new hope, and new direction marking the life of this great, old, downtown church. It is my intent in the pages that follow to share with you the elements of our story that have made the difference. We are persuaded that what happened at First Church in downtown Orlando is translatable to other churches in city centers, maybe even to your church.

The passage of scripture that has guided and directed everything we have done at First Church is 2 Corinthians 2:12–6:13. Paul, the great apostle and architect of the early church, laid out the blueprint for a church's powerful witness and work for Jesus Christ. We have deliberately built our own ministry around that passage. Why? Because Paul's words were delivered to a church in a tough situation. The circumstances faced by the church at Corinth were every bit as tough, demanding, and uncertain as those faced by downtown congregations in our time. Little wonder we have held so fast to the words of this inspired text. In fact, in my study Bible, the subheads for that passage, and the verses under each subhead constitute both a call to action and a game plan for a downtown church. Here is that blueprint:

A Triumphant Ministry	2:12-17
A Commended Ministry	3:1-6
A Ministry of Splendor	3:7-18
An Honest Ministry	4:1-6
A Tried Ministry	4:7-18
A Courageous Ministry	5:1-10
A Reconciling Ministry	5:11-21
A Suffering Ministry	6:1-13

Those are the subheads for our vision. You dig into the verses, apply what you find to your church, and then stand back! You are about to witness an explosion detonated by the Spirit of God.

One particular verse, 2 Corinthians 6:11, has become a kind of internal maxim for all of us who are professional staff and lay leaders in our congregation: "Our mouth is open to you, . . . our heart is wide" (RSV). At First Church our open mouths proclaim the good news of the gospel of Jesus Christ without reserve, without shame, and without apology.

Proclamation is first and foremost. Proclamation stands at the center of everything we do. But we also have wide hearts. We are now in a position to significantly address any human need that might be presented to us, and, believe me, because of our downtown location, those needs come to us like the never-ending waves on Florida's shores. We have open mouths and wide hearts. It is just that simple, though the ministry flowing out of those words is anything but simple.

It may help you if next I open my own heart and share with you part of my sacred journey that brought us to Orlando in 1982. One chapter of the journey began forty years ago. It seems like yesterday.

CHAPTER 1

IDENTITY:
Heart of the City

Somebody tore down our cross!

As part of our preparation for Holy Week each year, we place three large wooden crosses in front of our church. At the base of the central cross there is a quoted verse from the book of Lamentations, "Is it nothing to you, all who pass by?" (Lam. 1:12). The display is intended to be a visible reminder of the significance of the holiest week of the Christian year. Also, it is one more attempt on our part to emblazon the sign of the cross on the center of our city.

Frankly, I was surprised when, one day in the midst of Holy Week, someone called the church to tell us they had observed an individual walk along Church Street, stop to look at the cross, become agitated and enraged, and proceed to jump up on the huge wooden cross and tear it to the ground. A short while after the incident, I happened to pass by the front of the church as two of our staff people, Gene Wynbissinger and Damon Willow, were engaged in repairing the broken cross and replacing it in the ground. Damon paused long enough from his work to say to me, "You can tear down the cross, but you can't stop the Christ." They resumed their work and soon the cross was back in place.

That incident has percolated in my mind ever since. Of course I am reminded immediately of Paul's consistent declaration that while the cross of Jesus Christ is salvation to some, it is a stumbling block to others. The cross is winsome for us, but it is offensive to others. Therefore, while it may be difficult for me to understand how someone walking along the sidewalk in front of our church could become so angered by the sight of the cross that they would physically tear it down, I can at least understand there are those who do not wish to deal with the implications of that cross. When the cross becomes central in your life, it will change the way you live. You strive to become more and more like the Christ who died on that cross. Some people, for the life of them, cannot bring themselves to do that. For such people, the cross is a stumbling block.

By the same token, when the cross becomes central in a city, it begins to change that city. Some people, inevitably, will stand in opposition. Because the witness of a downtown church is as pronounced and visible as our cross placed on Church Street, the downtown church inevitably will face challenges to its existence. However, according to the way we think at First Church, that very fact is all the incentive we need to stay downtown in order to keep raising the sign of the cross and the banner of Christ and the message of faith. "You can tear down the cross, but you can't stop the Christ." If you cannot stop Christ, you cannot stop Christ's church, either. That is why, here on Church Street in downtown Orlando, we continue to offer to our city an open door, an open hand, and an open heart.

An Open Door

The doors of our church are open to all. The people in our congregation reflect a wide variety of backgrounds, geographical locations, denominational heritages, personal interests, and points of view on life in this world. Yet, we are bound together by one common thread: our love for Jesus. All people, no matter who they are, no matter what their circumstances may be, no matter what they may have been or done or said or thought in life, are welcome to partake of the love of Christ that permeates this place. No one is excluded.

An Open Hand

Millions of dollars are spent through the ministry of this church meeting human needs. Because of our location, we have the opportunity to serve people who are *down-and-out*, people who have bottomed-out in the business of living and have no place to turn. In downtown Orlando, our church is the place they go and they find an open hand, willing to secure for them what they need to keep body and soul together. Also, because of our location, we have the opportunity to serve those we might call *up-and-out*, the people who are a part of the business and professional community. We are surrounded, throughout the week, by thousands of people who make up this city's workforce. So many times, on the outside, these people seem to have everything, but, on the inside, they wonder if they instead have nothing. This church offers to them an open hand, encouraging them to find life's ultimate meaning in Jesus Christ. Our church cares.

An Open Heart

From the geographical heart of the city of Orlando, we strive to be a church that has an impact on the quality of life in this community. We strive to be a church that is engaged in the transformation of human lives, the building of significant relationships, and the fostering of biblical desires and ambitions. We strive to be a church where people can encounter Christ, learn the Scriptures, join in uplifting worship, experience a spirit of belonging, and give themselves away in the Spirit of the Lord. We strive to be a church where people learn that the power of love is infinitely greater than the love of power. We strive to be a church that dares to call a sin a sin and offers Christ in rebuttal. We strive to be a church waging war against loneliness, injustice, poverty, oppression, and anything else that diminishes the human spirit, devalues human life, and tarnishes the image of God in us all. We strive to be a church embracing our city with the love of Christ, believing that, in time and in turn, our city will embrace that same Christ. So here at the heart of the city, we have a heart for that city. And therein hangs a tale.

Sometimes the truth comes from the most unlikely places, and this time it was not only unlikely, it was also barely understandable.

Herb Haack was a German immigrant whose love for his adopted country (America), and his adopted city (Orlando), and his adopted church (First Church) knew no limits. His devotion both to Christ and to our church had earned for him the right to speak. However, the vestiges of his mother tongue made his communication in English a challenge to comprehend. So when Herb Haack stood that day to address our church, we all leaned forward, knowing we would have to pay special attention. Like E. F. Hutton, when Herb Haack spoke, people listened. And in Herb's case, listened hard.

The issue before us as a church was our commitment to stay downtown. To remain in that location would mean eventually needing to acquire the entire city block and everyone was reeling at the possibility of doing so. Herb Haack made an impassioned plea in favor of staying. He told of the time a number of years before when the Session (our governing board) had considered the same alternative. At that particular time, the church was growing in numbers and outgrowing the facilities. But also at that time, our church was surrounded by a number of homes that would be expensive to acquire. The church had the opportunity to purchase a pristine lakefront location north of the city. Ironically, the property was immediately adjacent to Herb Haack's place of business. Had the church moved to that location, the value of Herb's own holdings would have greatly appreciated. Yet, even though his position ran against his own best interest, he had strongly encouraged the church to remain downtown. And at that time, the church had voted to do so.

Now, confronted with the same decision provoked this time not by growing numbers but decreasing numbers, the church found itself locked in inconclusive debate. It was at that point that Herb Haack rose to his feet. Ben McKenney, our church administrator, recounts what happened next:

Herb's broken English, with a heavy European accent and dramatic style, was most impressive. Being from the "old world" one would expect that he would like for things to stay the same, and I guess in one sense, he did want things to be the same. He wanted us to honor our heritage of ministering to the heart of this city by remaining downtown. But the paradox was that he was also a progressive type of guy who was looking to the future. His strong evangelical faith convinced him that we could stay downtown and still grow. His argument was compelling, and we voted to stay put.

In a most memorable way, Herb Haack reminded us of the church's long history at our downtown location. But he also charged us to draw our sense of mission for the future from the realities of the past. It was a past that began in 1876. On March 18 of that year, eleven dedicated adults and their children banded together to form the First Presbyterian Church of Orlando. Thirteen years later, a frame building was completed on the southeast corner of Church and Main (now Magnolia) Streets, which is still the church's site. Over the next thirty years as increasing church membership reflected the growth of Orlando, the Presbyterians continued to add buildings to the site to accommodate the church's expanding ministry. In 1956, as the church celebrated its seventy-fifth anniversary, a new sanctuary was opened. The glorious history of First Church, so inextricably tied to the history of the city of Orlando, has been carefully documented and preserved for good reason. As our Heritage Committee states: "It is hard to negotiate the future unless one has framed clearly a memory of the past and an appreciation for it."

Identity

Herb Haack understood that truth. His speech delivered in broken English, but from a full heart, became the catalyst that provoked us to establish our church's identity. For out of our significant decision to remain downtown, we developed our church's identifying motto: The Heart of the City. When you call the church on the telephone, our receptionist always answers, "First Presbyterian Church, the heart of the city." The words, so frequently heard or read around our church campus, are not casually delivered. They are fraught with deep meaning. Churches are like people. They not only have names, they have an identity. My name, for example, is Howard Edington. But who I am is much more than simply my name. My identity as a person is framed by the roles or functions I perform in life: husband, father, minister, friend, to name a few. By the same token, our church is infinitely more than the name that appears on the sign out front. Our church's identity is determined by its location and its mission.

Spread out a map of the city of Orlando, stick a pin at the corner of Church Street and Magnolia Street, and you will see graphically displayed that First Church is the geographic center of the city. So physically speaking, we are the heart of the city. But much more important, the motto has a spiritual meaning. We believe that we are called to be Christ's heart for the city of Orlando. That is our identity.

From that sense of identity, we have developed two significant documents that are designed to help us live up to our claim of being the heart of this city. The first document is our mission statement. It reads as follows:

Our church's response to the call of God is to create, within the heart of the city, a community where people are confronted by the power of the gospel, and learn to live their lives through Christ in the world.

The one-sentence mission statement appears every week on the Sunday worship folder and on other publications produced by the church. It provides the intellectual and emotional energy we need to meet the challenges of our downtown location.

A second document referred to as "A Goal Statement" is equally important if not quite so visible. The Goal Statement governs the decision-making process flowing out of our Session. Here is that statement in its entirety:

We have a dream. We believe First Presbyterian Church of Orlando can become a *teaching church* of the Presbyterian Church, USA.

The concept of the *teaching hospital* and its impact upon the practice of medicine is an intriguing one. The teaching hospital provides the best patient care because it is able to develop the best staff and the best facilities. The teaching hospital also develops the areas of specialty to the fullest extent and because of the presence of interns and residents, the doctors in the teaching hospital have to stay abreast of the latest techniques and practice the highest quality of medicine. The result of these factors is a great hospital with outstanding medical care for the patients.

Is it possible that what a teaching hospital does for the practice of medicine, a teaching church could do for the Kingdom of God? How glorious it would be if the First Presbyterian Church of Orlando understood itself to be a teaching church where the various aspects of the ministry of the church were practiced and developed to the fullest extent, and where individuals of churches from other parts of the country could come to learn, not only through classroom experience, but also through practical application, how to do ministry in more effective ways. Therefore, those engaged in the practice of ministry here would, of necessity, have to hone their skills and gifts to near perfection, thus providing for the members of First Presbyterian Church of Orlando the highest quality of ministry.

What will it take for First Presbyterian of Orlando to become such a church? It will take vision. It will require the faith and the courage to build a strong staff, to draw lay people into ever more significant areas of the church's ministry, and to provide the finest facilities. It will mean providing exciting and participatory worship experiences. It will mean moving the church to the cutting edge of Christian education where new concepts of providing for spiritual growth will be developed. It will mean, not only finding needs in the community and meeting them, but also addressing the structures of society that create those human needs.

It will mean providing pastoral care that moves beyond the concept of visitation and crisis intervention, into the area of developing health and wholeness in individuals and families. It will mean providing a ministry that touches every aspect of the human experience, beginning, of course, with the spiritual, but moving into other areas as well, such as recreational development, cultural awareness, social opportunities, and intellectual growth.

It will mean creating such a web of interlocking human relationships that no one who is touched by First Presbyterian Church of Orlando need ever feel alone. It will mean using the media creatively to communicate the gospel. Ultimately, it will mean that when people in this country want to know what it means to be the church engaged in significant and faithful ministry to Jesus Christ, they will say, "Look at First Presbyterian Church of Orlando."

This is no idle dream. It is a goal within our reach. It is a vision possible. First Presbyterian Church of Orlando shall strive to become a teaching church of the Presbyterian Church, USA.

Paradoxically, nothing could be more lifeless than cold words printed on a dry page, but nothing could be more lively than the actions those words inspire. The Mission Statement and the Goal Statement are anything but lifeless words. In fact, like matches, when they are struck in our corporate life they ignite the flames of significant action. The decisions we make, the programs we conceive, the plans we develop, the ministries we wage, all draw lifeblood from those two statements. There is nothing particularly profound or poetic about the language. There is nothing unique or revolutionary about the concept. But those two statements, together with the motto "The Heart of the City," have become the identifying marks for our people. They understand what our mission is because they are constantly reminded of our identity and what we are all about as a result of our identity. A key element, then, in giving new life, new vision, and new direction to a downtown church is to establish that church's identity and to exalt it. For then the people of that church shall understand who they are and what they are to do in obedience to the lordship of Jesus Christ.

Viability

Of course identity in and of itself is not enough. Calling yourself "the Heart of the City" without demonstrating a viable ministry in the heart of the city is fruitless at best, futile at worst. Once we established our identity as a church, we then set out on a deliberate course to demonstrate our viability as a downtown congregation. Our first step was to secure enough property to guarantee our future. Downtown churches all over this country are being strangled to death by not having sufficient property to sustain a viable and vibrant ministry. The handwriting was on the wall, without additional property we would be shut out of the downtown action. It was not then, never has been, never will be, our intention to create a "landed kingdom" in downtown Orlando. We wanted only enough property to provide flexibility in meeting future demands and opportunities. There were three other parcels on the city block where our physical facility stands. One was a service station; one was a dirt lot used for parking by a neighboring bank; one was a funeral home.

We committed ourselves to the strategy of attempting to purchase those adjacent parcels and we committed the whole matter in prayer to the Lord. It was a leap of faith on the part of the congregation, as risky as any other act of faith in the history of the church. It turned out to be a very costly strategy in terms of dollars, but the dollar cost fades into insignificance when viewed from the perspective of succeeding years. For example, when we purchased the service station the cost was seventeen dollars per square foot. By the time we were able to purchase the third parcel, the funeral home, the cost had jumped to fifty-five dollars per square foot. We

had poured enormous sums of money into those three trans-
actions, and what did we have to show for it? My wife,
Trisha, used to jokingly insert a needle into me by saying,
"You've led these people to spend nearly three million dollars and all you've got to show for it is a nonfunctioning
service station, a decaying funeral home, and a dirt lot that
fills up with water every time it rains!" But all joking aside,
while that was all we did have, we also had a future. We
would never be forced to evacuate our downtown location.
We would now be able to handle any growth the Lord might
provide.

Here, then, is a cold, hard principle for the downtown
church: secure enough property to make the church's ministry viable. Beg or borrow (but don't steal!) the money. Spend
whatever time it takes, but get your holy hands on the
property you need. It will be worth the cost. Establishing our
identity and demonstrating our viability enabled us to turn
the corner from slow death to the first signs of new life. A
downward spiral in membership beginning in 1975, as documented in the statistics of our Presbyterian General Assembly, was reversed and the membership has increased every
year since.

Please do not make the mistake of thinking that our church
moved into a growth mode simply because we were in a
vital, dynamic city. Draw a circle with a radius of a thousand
feet from our church's location on Church Street, and that
circle will encompass four other churches. One of those
churches, First United Methodist Church, was described in
an article in *Christian Century* magazine as a church that, "has
not tasted the sweet numerical success enjoyed by evangeli-
cals outside the center city. Indeed its attendance at Sunday
services has declined precipitously since midcentury."[1] First
Baptist Church decided to move out of downtown and has
flourished in a new environment. A core group of that congregation did choose to remain downtown under the name
Downtown Baptist Church, and is engaged in a struggle to

grow larger and stronger. Saint Paul Lutheran Church completely abandoned the idea of a downtown church and transformed the property into a high-rise retirement home with a small chapel on the top. First Church of the Nazarene has chosen to minister primarily to its own people, does it extremely well, but remains small in numbers. Analyze what has happened here in Orlando and it becomes crystal clear that you cannot appeal to your surroundings as either a plus or a minus. It is not the environment of the community that makes the downtown church live or die. Rather it is the individual church's chosen sense of identity and calculated sense of mission. First Presbyterian Church of Orlando is a growing, expanding, thriving congregation not because of the city that surrounds it but because the congregation deliberately chose to uphold the banner of Christ at the center of the city, cost what it may.

Visibility

Identity and viability are two ingredients in a recipe for a successful downtown church. Visibility is the third ingredient, and we have come to believe it might be the most important of the three. Our congregation may understand who we are and we may have what we need to produce a viable ministry, but if the church is not visible in the larger community, then it cannot hope to thrive, perhaps not even to survive. A downtown church of necessity must draw people from a broad geographical region. Churches located out in residential areas will almost automatically be visible and attractive to people living in those areas. The downtown church on the other hand must work night and day to increase and enhance its visibility, thus drawing people from the outlying areas into downtown. First Church is known all over the region of Central Florida, not simply for its geographical location, but more important for the Christlike influence that it exercises in the community.

My guess is that if you were to ask the person on the street or the person in the pew what has made First Church most visible in this community, both would agree: television. As significant as television is today to the ministry of First Church, it was not a grand beginning. There were times of uncertainty and struggle.

Television had been a part of our ministry at First Presbyterian in Pine Bluff, Arkansas. There we had come to learn firsthand what a powerful force television can be for communicating the faith. Think about it. Historically the church has always used the most popular forms of communication for delivering the message of the gospel. Centuries ago Jerome startled the world by putting the Scriptures into the language of the people. Gutenberg's new invention, the printing press, churned out—what else, the Bible. Most of us would be hard-pressed to recall anything that happened during the reign of King James in England save his authorization of the Bible translation that carries his name. In our own time, television, the most powerful and popular communication medium of the age, provides us with a matchless opportunity to put the message of the gospel within reach of virtually every human being. Armed with my deep conviction that the church must take advantage of the television opportunity, and with the years of experience on television in Arkansas, I hoped and prayed that the same opportunity would be available in Orlando.

Prior to our moving, Ches Magruder, a member of First Church, wrote me a letter sharing his desire to underwrite a television ministry. He had selfish reasons for doing so, he said. His spouse was frail, unable to get to church, and he could see the possibility of television bringing their church into their home. He immediately began negotiations with a local television station.

God's will is sometimes very clear to me; other times not so very clear. This was one time when clarity was lacking. As the movers were placing the furniture in our new home in

Orlando, the church called to say that Mr. Magruder had died quite suddenly. Before officially beginning work as the minister of First Church, I conducted Ches Magruder's funeral. What hopes and dreams we may have had for a television ministry seemed to die as well. The benefactor was gone. What to do? Do you remember the lesson from the Preface of this book to "stir what you got"? Mr. Magruder's estate was placed in the charge of five trustees, prominent persons in our community and our church. I shared with them the letter I had received from Mr. Magruder and in response they developed a plan. At first I was not enamored of the plan, but I came to appreciate its wisdom. Their plan was to underwrite a television ministry over a three-year period of time with the trustees' gift being reduced by one-third each year so that gradually the church would assume full responsibility. Their wisdom both encouraged and enabled the church to become immersed in the television ministry and thus to "own" it. Looking back, it is obvious that the success of the television ministry grew directly out of our congregation's sense of ownership.

The television ministry at our church has two dimensions: separate approaches, same purpose. One dimension we call *The Certain Sound* ministry. Borrowing its name from 1 Corinthians 14:8 (KJV), "For if the trumpet gives an uncertain sound, who shall prepare himself to the battle?" *The Certain Sound* is a weekly telecast of portions of our worship service, particularly the sermon. We operate on the principle of "eavesdropping." Since our first commitment is to the congregation seated in our sanctuary, discreetly placed television cameras simply "eavesdrop" on the service. The service is taped, edited down to a thirty-minute program, and telecast on the following Sunday morning.

There are three advantages to this method.

1. The one-week delay allows us to edit the tape for the television audience. We recognize the vast difference between experiencing worship in our sanctuary and watching

a worship service on a television screen. The live service is designed for worshipers in that room. The edited version is designed for the television audience.

2. The discreetly placed cameras preserve a worshipful atmosphere in our sanctuary.

3. The thirty-minute time slot is much less costly to purchase than would be a one-hour slot.

The Certain Sound is underwritten by the operating budget of our church, removing the need for on-the-air fund-raising and permitting a pure presentation of the gospel out of the context of Christian worship. In addition to confronting unchurched people with the claims of Christ, a blessed by-product of *The Certain Sound* has been its impact on believers both in our church and in other churches who, for whatever reason, are not able to be physically present in a church on Sunday morning. Furthermore, we have discovered from the volume of mail received that there are numbers of people in our community who will not enter a church sanctuary, who regard television as their primary contact point with the church, and consequently, who have come to regard me as their pastor and First Church as their "virtual church." They support us with gifts and contributions and, if asked, would consider First Church their church, though they may never have passed through its doors. This last group constitutes a phenomenon deserving of serious study by church consultants and deserves a more in-depth response than we at First Church, up to now, have been able to offer.

The second dimension is the *television spots* ministry. This is geared to that large segment of population who will not stop their channel surfing for a thirty-minute sermon. The spots, more than sixty of which we have produced and aired, are thirty seconds long and are played at strategically determined times on both network and cable channels. We filmed them in a wide variety of places and settings, ranging from the shores of local beaches, to the Rocket Garden at Cape

Canaveral, to the Capitol building in Washington, D.C. As Paul taught in 1 Corinthians 3:5-7, it is our job to plant God's seed of the gospel as well as to water it; but it is God, not us, who makes the seed grow. The television spots, designed to plant the seeds of the gospel in the hearts of the non-churched, accomplish the following:

❑ **The spots provide a nonthreatening, noncoercive, and nonmanipulative proclamation of the gospel in simple, timeless terms.** As Christ often taught in the marketplace simple spiritual truths in the form of parables, we seek to follow his teaching method through spots that take ordinary, contemporary settings and circumstances and draw from them spiritual messages. One of my favorite spots was filmed in the neonatal unit of a local hospital. In my arms was a brand new child. The text:

There's nothing like holding a newborn baby. You look at your little bundle of life and realize that a huge miracle has occurred. Here is a tiny little person of unlimited potential. Then, suddenly, the thought hits you: "Who will teach my baby how to make it through life? And who will serve as a role model?" Take a look in the mirror. You, the parents, will have the biggest influence on your baby's future. Scary, isn't it? But it's not so terrifying to parents who can admit to their son or daughter, "I am a child, too. A child of God. God is my ultimate role model, and he should be yours, too." So hug your baby and be confident that God has given this child to you, and then offer your child's future to God.

❑ **The spots are designed to evangelize, not to advertise.** We do not use repetitive product sales techniques and do not expect that which results from such techniques. Television is a powerful tool that we dare not misuse by manipulating people and compromising the gospel. The spots seek to project grace that is irresistible to the human heart. The hook of the spots is that there is no hook, just the Word of God.

❑ **The spots provoke action.** They provide a springboard for personal evangelism for our members, as well as other believers in the community, who are given the opportunity to discuss the messages of the spots with non-Christian friends or associates who happen to catch the spots on television.

❑ **The spots highlight Christ and the values of the spiritual life, not our church and its ministry.** At the end of each spot a graphic overlay containing the name of our church appears briefly on the screen. It is nothing more than a subtle and tasteful reminder of where the spots originated. But the message takes clear priority over the messenger.

The spots have created positive visibility for our church in the community. Even Greg Dawson, the television critic of *The Orlando Sentinel*, has taken note. He writes:

Edington's 30-second sound bites for Christ (are) an attempt to encourage folks who would not normally think about going to church to see that the spiritual dimension is all around us and is very much a part of what we are. Edington is well-known to those who watch an edited version of the First Presbyterian service that airs Sunday mornings at 9 on Channel 9, but that is preaching to the choir. The primetime spots are aimed at a general audience that has never seen Edington in his vestments. . . . While the artistic merit of the spots may be debatable, one thing seems undeniable: they work. Of the 400 or so people who join FPC each year, 25-30 percent indicate on questionnaires that they come as a direct result of the TV spots. A business would consider that a spectacular return on its advertising dollar. Even more notable than the number of new members is the demographic—"a significant number of young singles and young couples," Edington says. "For an old established downtown church like ours to be absolutely awash in young children and parents is amazing."[2]

Some Christians in our time question the use of television as an arm of ministry. We would be the first to acknowledge that the television airwaves and the money television can generate have drawn self-serving charlatans to television evangelism. However, rather than writing off the opportunity because there are those who abuse it, we believe that a television ministry with integrity has a place. Our particular approach to the use of television upholds:

1. **My personal integrity.** I receive no financial reward from the television ministry at all.

2. **The integrity of our congregation.** It does not compromise the atmosphere of worship for those who sit on our pews.

3. **The integrity of our faith.** The gospel is presented pure, unadorned, without appeals for money.

Let's pull this discussion out of the realm of the conceptual into realm of the practical, or hard, cold numbers. On any given weekend, some 200,000 people are watching *The Certain Sound* in Central Florida, a hundred times more than the number listening to the sermon in the sanctuary. On any given weekend, we have 275 to 300 visitors in worship. The majority of those visitors have found their way to our doors because they were first introduced to us by television.

At First Church we have come to appreciate television as the most powerful communication tool of our time. While it can seem frightfully expensive, careful planning and market research combined with creative thinking can reduce the cost somewhat. Believe me when I tell you, though, it is definitely a cost worth paying. Nothing has heightened our church's visibility in the community as has television. Nothing has helped us reach out to the thousands upon thousands of unchurched people in Orlando as has television. The outreach and visibility television provides has been a direct and daily contributor to this church's growth curve.

Leaders from our community consistently acknowledge our visibility. Linda Chapin, Orange County Chair and one of our most powerful political leaders, speaking at the formal opening of our church's Clayton Life Center, said:

I have a very clear recollection of the day that Dr. Edington and Joan Ruffier and Ben McKenney came to talk to me about the vision you had for this church, here in the heart of downtown Orlando. The reason that recollection is so very clear is because I also remember how deeply touched and moved I was, and am today, by the vision of what this church and its urban ministry can mean, and will mean, to the people of this community. It is an extraordinary task which you have undertaken, and I know that there must have been times when you wondered if your dreams must have been too big. Yet look at what you have accomplished. Look how far you have come. Please know and believe what it is going to mean to this community. As time goes by, I realize more and more that there are heroes and heroines in our everyday lives and I believe an awful lot of them are in this church. So I am here to say, on behalf of the rest of the people out there, thank you for what you are trying to do, and thank you for what you *will* accomplish."

The church's impact on the community outside its walls is further reflected in a commentary broadcast entitled, "A Tribute to First Presbyterian" by Gene Burns, a popular radio talk-show host and writer. He said:

In the several years I have been writing these commentaries and conducting talk programs on this radio station and others, I've had occasion to be critical of churches which, in my opinion, fail to fully follow the dictates of the Judeo-Christian moral code. I've taken a decidedly dim view of houses of worship that are content to be gathering places for self-professed saints and not refuges for sinners. Churches that lay claim to the Christian traditions, specifically, often seem unsure of just what the Gospels require of good stewards. Since I have been critical so often, perhaps I bear a greater burden than many to draw to your attention a church that I believe represents the very best that could be expected of those of us who inhabit the temporal, and hence imperfect, realm. As I frequently am, I was faced recently with a request to find assistance for an elderly lady in Orlando. The lady's problem simply did not fit the carefully drawn preconceptions of the existing social service agencies. In short, she was falling through the cracks of the highly touted safety net. Finally in exasperation, I asked Dr. Howard Edington, pastor of the First Presbyterian Church, whom I have come to admire and respect, if he knew of a solution. I am delighted to report that the problem was dealt with swiftly and expertly by Dr. Edington and a special interdisciplinary committee of lay volunteers that the First Presbyterian Church has developed. To the best of my knowledge, this existing effort has received no publicity and no community recognition, perhaps by design. But it deserves both. So I tip my hat to a Christian community that has demonstrated a keen understanding of the imperatives of the Gospels, a community that has found the fulcrum that balances personal salvation and social conscience. Not only is Howard Edington a stunningly effective preacher, but there is now dramatic evidence that his congregation has heard him.

But perhaps I did not fully understand our church's visibility in this community until tragedy struck my own family. When our son, John David, was killed in an automobile accident just four days before Christmas in 1994, the story was carried both in the newspaper and on the local television channels, over and over again for a full week, interviewing family, friends, and church staff members, and covering portions of worship services being held throughout Christmas week and Christmas Day in relationship to John David's death. That extensive coverage forced us to deal with our personal grief in a public manner. While that was terribly painful for us, there was a measure of grace in it all.

John David's accident on a rain-slick road was no different from any number of automobile accidents in our community. What was different was his tie to the prominently visible ministry of the First Church. Media attention focused on his death triggered a veritable avalanche of grief, concern, affection, and encouragement from people all over the city, hundreds upon hundreds of them, many of whom we had not known personally. Of course, we were grateful for the expressions of sympathy that we received from great leaders nationally, such as President Clinton, Ruth and Billy Graham, Vonette and Bill Bright (members of our congregation who were among the first at our sides that tragic morning), and Arvella and Robert Schuller. But what struck us so deeply, frequently moving us to tears, were the gestures that came from so many people in our city whose names we did not know or whom we knew only by their first names and so they identified themselves by their function: a young man who had waited our table at a restaurant earlier that week; our letter carrier; the young woman who sells peanuts in the section where we sit at the Orlando Magic games; a woman who had hung some wallpaper for us months before the accident; the mechanic at the garage where our car had been serviced.

As our hearts were breaking we discovered that their hearts were breaking too. Why? Because somehow the ministry of this church and my own personal ministry had become so interwoven into the fabric of this community's life that multiple hundreds of people not on the membership rolls of our church (in fact many were members of other churches in the community or members of no church at all) felt that somehow our church was theirs and I was, in some sense, a pastor to them. Clearly it was that kind of feeling that enabled them to have the courage and the compassion to reach out to me and my family in our time of need.

To be sure, over the years I had encountered the impact of the church's visibility in a variety of ways. I rarely shop at a mall, or eat at a restaurant, or go to a movie, or walk the downtown streets without being approached by people whose life has been touched for good by the ministry of our church. This so-called fishbowl existence affects not only me and the church, but our entire family. Some people regard the personal impact of such visibility as being negative. Some ministers have unlisted home phones, but mine is in the book. Some ministers guard their personal lives as closely as soldiers guard the gold in Fort Knox, but I want my people to feel that they know me on a deeply personal level. Some ministers' families deeply resent living in a "fishbowl" and fight against it for all they are worth, but my family is different. While my family has experienced the negative impact, they also recognize the potential value of the visibility.

Among a rather extensive collection of writings in John David's personal effects, we found a school essay of his in which he articulated the difficulties of living in a "fishbowl," but ultimately confirmed its values. Here is how he ended what he wrote:

I don't think it would be honest of me to have you thinking that my life is so bad. I would much prefer to attempt to convince you of the positive aspect of living in a "fishbowl": I am so often in the presence of people who have made a commitment to making the world a better place to live, and who are more concerned about things that are truly important—stewardship, hunger, world peace, loving our environment—than whether you have long hair and wear an earring.

Yes, he, at one point in his young life, had both long hair and an earring, and undoubtedly had encountered the negative dimension of his father's and his church's visibility. By God's grace he had come to terms with it and wound up claiming it as a positive force in his life.

So it has been in a wonderful twist of the Lord's irony that the very visibility that directly produced growth for our downtown church became for me and for my family a healing force in our time of greatest need. The church's identity helped me to maintain my own.

CHAPTER 11

INTENTION:
We're Here for Life

"God moves in wondrous ways, his mysteries to perform."

I know you think I wrote that incorrectly. I did not. I wrote what I meant, and I meant what I wrote. The old hymn is true: "God moves in a mysterious way, his wonders to perform." But it is equally true when you flip-flop the language. We have seen firsthand the wondrous ways God chooses and uses to perform his mysteries in the downtown church. Frankly what has happened at First Church over the last decade is a mystery. I cannot explain it. I cannot account for it. I certainly cannot take credit for it. It is as if God, for some mysterious reason, said, "I'm going to do something new in that old downtown church that may prove a blessing to other churches in other downtowns."

In 1984, when we made the commitment to remain downtown and developed a plan for purchasing the property adjacent to us, our people were called to take an extraordinary step of faith. We had no funds in reserve and no plans for a capital campaign. Suddenly, the service station property on the southwest corner of our block became available. If we did not move quickly and decisively, the opportunity would be lost and our dreams of remaining downtown would be dealt a potentially fatal blow. Our lay leaders, with no visible means of support, save their reliance upon God, voted to purchase the property. The price? $350,000—money we did not have, money we had no prospect of receiving. As we struggled with that decision, various members of our

Session kept repeating Proverbs 29:18: "Where there is no vision, the people perish" (KJV). A person with no vision, no sense of compelling purpose in life, is a person destined for a dead-end experience. Likewise, a church with no vision, no sense of who it is and what it is all about, is a church not likely to arrive at a significant destination. No vision, no life. T. B. Matson once said, "Christians who have turned the world upside down for God have been men and women with a vision in their hearts and a Bible in their hands." It is true! If there is no vision, no dream to drive us, no goal to draw our best energies, no horizon to summon us, then there is no hope and no life. Thankfully our elders had a vision in their hearts and a Bible in their hands, and they took a step that practical wisdom and good business sense would have decreed as foolish. They were able to do something because they believed something and believed it deeply.

The Master's Plan

As often happens when you embark upon a journey of faith, God meets you on the way. So it was for us. Wonder of wonders, God answered our act of faith with his own act of grace. He acted through a most unusual and remarkable woman.

She called my office asking for an appointment to see me, declining to tell my secretary the reason for the request. When Laureda Stuart came into my office that day, I knew her only by her name on my appointment book. Obviously advanced in years, she walked unsteadily with a cane, her clothing out of date and mismatched.

Without benefit of pleasantries, she said, "Sit down in your chair. I want to sit across the desk and talk to you." Taken aback, I sat down in my chair and proceeded to behold the unfolding wonder of God.

She said, "I haven't met you. I prefer to stay in the background. I love to hear you preach, but I sit in the back and I don't greet you at the door."

Having no earthly idea where this conversation was heading, I said, because I couldn't think of anything else to say, "Thank you for your encouragement."

She made no response to my comment. She simply placed her elbows on my desk, looked me straight in the eye, and said, "I hate interest!"

Somewhat baffled, I queried, "Ma'am?"

She said, "You heard me. I hate interest!"

Now I was really confused. I could not imagine what in the world this unusual older woman was doing sitting in my office repeating her definite refrain, "I hate interest!"

I said, "Mrs. Stuart, I don't know that I understand what you are saying."

Now she was practically in my face. "I told you I hate interest!"

"Yes ma'am, I understand that, but I don't know what that has to do with me."

She said, "I'll tell you what it has to do with you."

By this time, I began to think that I was engaged in a debate that I did not understand and was destined to lose. My bewilderment was expressed in silence.

The silence did not stop her. Even more forcefully than before she said, "I love this church. It has come to my attention that you have led this church to borrow money from the bank to purchase the service station on the corner. We are paying interest on that money, and I hate interest."

"Aha," I thought to myself, "now I understand what this debate is about, but still I am going to lose it. She is going to give me a withering blast for getting the church into debt."

But suddenly her demeanor changed. Her voice softened a bit. She said, "Since I hate interest, I don't like the idea that my church is paying interest. So what I want to do is write a little check to help out on the note and cut down on that interest."

She then reached down into a burgundy crushed-velvet purse that looked as if it had been retrieved from the bargain barrel at the thrift shop. While she was so engaged, I found myself thinking, "Thank goodness, she is not going to take me to task, and I will be grateful for any little gift she can give."

She pulled out her checkbook and began writing a check, all the while repeating her refrain, "I do hate interest." She tore the check out of the book, shoved it across to me, and said, "Preacher, I hope this helps."

I picked up the check, glanced at it, and suddenly found my head swimming, my heart pounding, and my hand shaking. The check was for $350,000! I could not believe it, at least not at first. Then my faith kicked in, and I could believe it after all. Wonder of wonders, God had used Laureda Stuart to confirm for us that we were doing precisely what God had wanted us to do.

As all of these thoughts exploded in my brain, she then pierced my reverie with these words, "There is one condition to this gift." As quickly as my heart had soared only moments before, it came quickly crashing back to earth. Weakly I stammered out, "And what would the condition be?" dreading to hear the reply. She said, "I told you earlier I love to hear you preach, but my legs are bad. I can't walk far. Do you think I could have a reserved parking place close to the church?" Believe you me, she had her parking space twenty-four hours later!

Calculating the psychological impact that had upon our congregation is all but impossible. Suffice it to say, we took it for what it was—a sign from God. And we began to build a vibrant ministry downtown. We experienced years of unprecedented growth. As the decade of the 90s began, we were bursting at the seams with people and programs. Our physical facilities were taxed almost to the breaking point. Once again, our lay leaders began to quote Proverbs 29:18: "Where there is no vision, the people perish."

We then embarked upon the most ambitious long-range planning and construction project our church had ever tackled. Our mission was to be visionary, and the approach we took was to focus on what we wanted to be in our dreams (dreams can come true!) in ten years.

The Master Plan

The best way for me to communicate what transpired in the development of our Master Plan is to give voice to four key people who helped to make it happen. I posed the questions to them, and they responded. First, let me introduce you to the four so you may learn from their experiences:

Bob Lovvorn chaired the Long-Range Planning Committee. He built a wonderful career selling class rings to high school and college students, but now he spends all of his time "selling" the faith. And, oh, what a wonderful job he does!

Bud Brakmann served as chief of the Implementation Task Force. His long years as a key player in the research and development division of the Martin Marietta Corporation were simply God's way of preparing him for his greatest project, the Master Plan at First Presbyterian.

Jim Hewitt headed the development of the financial plan and chaired the fund-raising campaign. He is one of Orlando's most prominent and admired businessmen, and his business acumen is outstripped only by his unabashed love for Jesus.

Marilyn King chaired the Building Committee. Her artistic flair, design expertise, and impeccable taste were offered as a gift to God and to our church; as a result, wherever you look at First Church you see her touch. But now, let them speak for themselves.

What happened when the growth began to spurt?

Lovvorn: We suddenly began having remarkable "luck," for the Lord obviously decided we had what it takes, and God began opening one door after another. We seemed to move through a sequence of miracles. Every obstacle fell one by one. The two remaining pieces of property not owned by us on our block became available to us one at a time, and the money came in to acquire each piece debt free. Once it became clear that we could control our destiny, our Session appointed the Long-Range Planning Committee and gave us a deadline.

Brakmann: The Planning Committee needed to be larger than normal practice would dictate. Ours numbered eleven. This was to include all the disciplines (legal, financial, technical, management, and government interface) that are involved. As a bonus, this resulted in a broader representation of the congregation, which turned out to be helpful later on during the "selling" phase. The more people who are in on the whole process, the better it is as time goes on.

How did the plan develop?

Lovvorn: The work of the Long-Range Planning Committee entailed: doing an assessment of every building and program on our block; surveying all parking within a mile of us; meeting with the city officials to see what their plans included; interviewing each departmental manager, lay leader, and staff person, together with a nucleus of church members in all of the programmed areas of the church (we wanted to know what their dreams were for ten years into the future with regards to programs and facilities); identifying new ministry desires, needs, and problems; and adhering to a strict schedule of periodic progress of reporting to the Session.

Brakmann: It was also important to talk to other churches; you can never get too smart. We looked for dimensions of work in other churches that might be duplicated in ours, but much more important perhaps, we looked for things we didn't want to do, or mistakes we didn't need to make.

Hewitt: We actually traveled to several other large churches to see how they had handled both their planning and their construction projects. While none of those other churches were downtown locations, we did pick up information that proved helpful to us. For example, we learned from examining the experience of other churches that we did not wish to get into a project that would incur long-term financing.

Lovvorn: We then collated all of the information we had derived and began to translate the dreams expressed by literally hundreds of people in our congregation into facts and figures. That report went to the Session, the Session unanimously approved it, and then assigned the task of making the dream come true to what we chose to call the Implementation Task Force.

How was the plan implemented?

Brakmann: The work of the Implementation Task Force was intense. The committee met every single week for a year and a half. As hard as this was, it was the only way to get through all that had to be done without dragging it out so long that the program changed and the congregation lost interest because nothing appeared to be happening. Ultimately, we developed a construction plan that would unfold in four phases with each phase standing on its own. The project was designed to accommodate the realities of construction in a downtown location.

Hewitt: We also made the decision to take a different tack in the actual construction, pursuing a "design/build concept" rather than a fixed-price contract. A fixed-price contract would be fine if the project were of a simple cookie-cutter type situation, where it would be easy to identify exactly what you want to build, and then put it out to bid for contractors. However, due to the fact that we were planning a very complex building plan covering four phases over an eight-to-ten year period, with a total expenditure exceeding $20 million, it was much wiser to utilize the "design/build concept." That particular concept has three key ingredients. In fact, it is similar to the "three-legged stool" plan I employ in my own spiritual life.

Each leg in the spiritual plan represents a spiritual area for growth. One leg of the stool covers your prayer time; one leg covers your study time; the third leg covers your worship time. In the "design/build concept" we tie together both the spiritual and the secular in the three-legged stool image. The first leg of the stool represents the church, the second leg represents the contractor, and the third leg represents the architect. The three legs working together in unity, with the Lord controlling the effort, is by far the best approach to use to assure the very best finished product at the most reasonable cost for the Lord's kingdom here on earth.

Brakmann: Of course even with this concept, a formal selection process should be followed in determining both architect and contractor. Our process included the following: written announcement or solicitation, qualification summary, written request for proposal, formal briefing, question and answer process, proposal submittal, and structured evaluation process.

Hewitt: Ultimately, having followed that process, we made our choices and the "design/build concept" not only became a reality, but proved to be a tremendous blessing for the church as the project began to unfold.

King: My job was to chair the Building Committee, which was a smaller version of the Implementation Task Force. Our task was to track progress and cost on a weekly basis and deal with issues associated with the construction project. The construction was significant enough so that the church administrator or a volunteer could not handle the role of project manager. Therefore, we hired a project manager to represent the church on the "design/build" team, and guided by his recommendations the committee made the decisions regarding the construction details, aesthetic considerations, and budget oversight.

Were there any negatives?

Lovvorn: In any visionary effort of this magnitude there will be some who are opposed and some who are *strongly* opposed to the project. They serve a useful purpose by forcing explanation and justification. So we always have tried to view opposition as an opportunity.

Brakmann: The opposition was usually expressed in the form of red herrings: sometimes intentional, but more often subconscious questions about the cost, concerns about investing in bricks instead of people, speculation that growth projections were wrong, or questions about what happens if the senior minister leaves. Scratch deep in those concerns, and the real issue is almost always the same, "We don't like change; we like it the way it used to be." Therefore, we had to keep stressing the vision, the benefits, and the purpose for it all as the plan unfolded.

Lovvorn: I think there will always be people who question the growth of a church, yet there seems to be immeasurably more power and strength for changing lives in a congregation of 9,000 than in forty-five congregations of 200. Keeping that focus in the forefront enabled us to deal with the relatively minor negativism that came our way.

What are the results?

Hewitt: As chair of the Fund-Raising Committee, I can tell you that we proceeded to explore various ways of raising funds and educating our membership. We embarked upon a significant capital campaign, and as a result of the tireless efforts on the part of many, we ended up raising over $9 million to cover the $7 million budgeted to complete the first phase of the building program. Once the Lord parted the Red Sea for us (figuratively speaking) by obtaining approval from the Session and the congregation to proceed with Phase 1, we were successful in obtaining a $6 million unsecured line of credit at prime rate. (Only Jesus Christ himself could pull this off, and he did!) The purpose of the credit line was to provide funding for the construction phase until the pledges came in to repay the line. Thus, we were able to construct Phase 1, the Life Center, without encumbering our church property.

King: That building is not only an architectural marvel, it is an example of true Christian community. Community, for me, is a place where people connect with one another under the lordship of Christ, and that's what happens in the Life Center. We have programs there for children, for older adults, and for Alzheimer's sufferers. We have a vast array of recreational opportunities for people of all ages. We now have the opportunity for a complete after-school ministry for our own children and youth, and the children and youth of the community. It is a place where they can receive tutoring help and work on computers to enhance their academic skills. It is a place where they can engage in physical activity and recreation. It is a place where they can be drawn into Bible study groups and grow in their faith experience. It is a place where they can receive instruction in music and the arts. The building is a building that lives. It lives in traditional hours, and in nontraditional hours, and in all kinds of ways. And to think it's just the first step—the first phase in a plan that will have an indelible impact on the city of Orlando.

Lovvorn: Let me tell you how I see it. Jack Welch, CEO of General Electric, writes in his book, *Control Your Own Destiny or Someone Else Will*, "If we have the right people in the right place at the right time, we win!" This is secular; however, I believe that God did this for us—the right people at the right place at the right time for God!

Mastering the Plan

As the Master Plan began to come into focus, we recognized the need for a way of communicating our hopes, dreams, and intentions to the congregation. Wonder of wonders, God's revealing hand was at work once more. My wife, Trisha, and I were visiting with her family in Shreveport,

Louisiana, for several days. Whenever we get that close to the location of our first pastorate, Kilgore, Texas, we never pass up the opportunity to visit with our friends there. One afternoon, as we left Shreveport for the one-hour drive to Kilgore, we were discussing the plans and the dreams taking place in Orlando, wondering how we could capture the imaginations of the people in our congregation. Trisha commented that she had just seen a sign that read, "We're here for life," and she remarked what a good slogan that would be, with its double meaning of life abundant and life forever. "We'd better go back to see what that was on," I said, quickly getting off at the next exit and retracing our journey of the past ten minutes. We never saw that sign again. We have no idea of its origin. How can I explain that? I cannot. I would not even try. God works in wondrous ways indeed. He delivered to us the slogan we needed for our present and future plans at First Church. "We're Here for Life" captures the three-faceted message required to convince our congregation of our long-term intention and to inspire them to the sacrifices necessary to make the dreams come true.

First, there is the message of **joy.** One of the great teachings derived from our Presbyterian catechism is "What is the chief end of man? To glorify God, and enjoy Him forever." Presbyterians tend to put more emphasis on the glorifying than on the enjoying. But we do not do that at First Church. We glorify God, and we do it in splendid Presbyterian style, but we also enjoy God—oh, do we ever! When we declare that "We're Here for Life," we are referring in part to the abundant life that Christ, alone, can bring. Jesus said in John 10:10, "I came that they may have life, and have it abundantly." Here at First Church we are committed to offering people the joy and the abundance of living life in Jesus Christ.

The second message is one of **permanence.** When we say "We're Here for Life," we mean that we are here for your lifetime. We are going to stay downtown and we are going to be here as far into the future as any of us can see. If you join First Church you don't have to worry about going any-where else. You will be going to this church, right here on this block, for as long as you live—unless the Lord returns first. We are committed to that kind of permanence.

The third message is one of **longevity.** Most churches that have achieved effectiveness in our time have been blessed by long pastorates. As Lyle Schaller puts it, "The larger the size of the congregation, the more likely that much of the conti-nuity is in the person of the senior minister."[1] The consis-tency and the security provided by an extended pastorate actually carries even more weight in the downtown church. As we were unfolding preliminary plans to the congregation, we repeatedly received the question, "Is Howard Edington going to stay here to see this through?" I am not so foolish as to believe in my indispensability to this church, but that repeated sentiment from our people was a way of asking for the consistency and the security they needed to embark upon such a dramatic venture. Therefore, when we say, "We're Here for Life," it carries a personal message from me: I am here for life! Never underestimate the power of the stated commitment to a long-term pastorate.

Therefore, the phrase "We're Here for Life" became the watchword for the Master Plan, which declares to our city that we are not going anywhere. Our whole city knows that we *are* here for life. That is a critical message to deliver. When a downtown church says, "We are going to wage a ministry in the name of Jesus Christ right here in the middle of this city whatever that might cost," that becomes a magnetic force drawing people into the church. We have learned with in-controvertible proof that God does indeed work in won-drous ways, his mysteries to perform.

We're here for life!

CHAPTER III

INVESTMENT:
The Chicken Salad Strategy

How do we increase the Master's return on his 120-year investment at First Church? Make no mistake, God will return to seek a return on his investment. The question the gospel poses is, "Will we have multiplied what God has entrusted to us?" Surely you recognize the image as drawn from Matthew 25 and Jesus' parable of the talents:

"For it is as if a man, going on a journey, summoned his slaves and entrusted his property to them; to one he gave five talents, to another two, to another one, to each according to his ability. Then he went away. The one who had received the five talents went off at once and traded with them, and made five more talents. In the same way, the one who had the two talents made two more talents. But the one who had received the one talent went off and dug a hole in the ground and hid his master's money. After a long time the master of those slaves came and settled accounts with them. Then the one who had received the five talents came forward, bringing five more talents, saying, 'Master, you handed over to me five talents; see, I have made five more talents.' His master said to him, 'Well done, good and trustworthy slave; you have been trustworthy in a few things, I will put you in charge of many things; enter into the joy of your master.' And the one with the two talents also came forward, saying, 'Master, you handed over to me two talents; see, I have made two more talents.' His master said to him, 'Well done, good and trustworthy slave; you have been trustworthy in a few things, I will put you in charge of many things; enter into the joy of your master.' Then the one who had received the one talent also came forward, saying, 'Master, I knew that you were a harsh man, reaping where you did not sow, and gathering where you did not scatter seed; so I was afraid, and I went and hid your talent in the ground. Here you have what is yours.' But his master replied, 'You wicked and lazy slave! You knew, did you, that I reap where I did not sow, and gather where I did not scatter? Then you ought to have invested my money with the bankers, and on my return I would have received what was my own with interest. So take the talent from him, and give it to the one with the ten talents. For to all those who have, more will be given, and they will have an abundance; but from those who have nothing, even what they have will be taken away. As for this worthless slave, throw him into the outer darkness, where there will be weeping and gnashing of teeth.' " Matthew 25:14-30.

The message of the parable cuts two ways. First, it reminds us that those to whom much is given, of them is much expected and much is required. Those who dare to expand the Master's investment, to them will more be given. But let us also remember that the parable teaches that those who horde and shepherd what they have been given, and do nothing more with the gifts of God's that are theirs, ultimately land in the place "where there will be weeping and gnashing of teeth." I do not exactly know what that means, but I do not care to find out. At First Church we came to recognize that the Lord had made an enormous investment in us. We were determined then, and we are determined still, to give God a most favorable return on that investment.

We knew the commitment to remain downtown would be expensive, but I doubt we knew how expensive until the Master Plan began to unfold. Our lay leaders recognized that it would take an extraordinary effort on our part and the supernatural intervention of the Lord to bring the Master Plan to fruition. Sensing the need to both anticipate and address concerns that might arise within the congregation at the prospect of tackling such an enormous challenge, our Session adopted seven operating principles to govern the development of the plan. The principles were designed to clear away concerns, but more than that, they were designed to keep us from faulty decision making that could prove disastrous.

Operating Principles

1. We shall not incur permanent financing for the church in the implementation of this plan. To the extent that a short-term "construction" loan is needed during the development of any phase, said loan must be fully backed by funds pledged to be received prior to the maturity date of the loan. The normal work and worship of our congregation will not be interrupted and worship services will not be relocated off-site, although it is understood that there will be times when we are inconvenienced.

2. We will work in harmony with and complementary to the plans of the city of Orlando.

3. Simultaneous with the unfolding phases of the plan here on Church Street, we shall be engaged in significant undertakings for other parts of Christ's kingdom locally, nationally, and internationally.

4. "On-site" benevolent ministries will be an integral part of our planning.

5. The plan has been, and will continue to be, developed by the lay leadership of the church. Consultation with the various ministries of the church, plus the general membership, will be a vital part of the implementation process.

6. The timetable for implementing the plan will remain flexible, with decision points established for each phase.

7. All construction and renovation projects included in the plan will maintain the architectural integrity of the buildings already in existence.

We then embarked upon a $21 million building program that would prepare us to provide a full-orbed ministry to Orlando in the twenty-first century. The program would unfold in four phases. Each phase could stand alone, enabling us to progress at a pace commensurate both with our needs and our ability to underwrite it, or stop at any juncture along the way should growth projections fail to materialize. The genius of the plan was that it would never jeopardize the quality of our day-to-day ministry or our future by locking us into a plan that must be completed as a whole in order to be effective. The complete plan, phase by phase, is detailed below (the architect's "footprint" accompanies this text).

Phase One, the life center: Newly completed, this 67,000 square-foot structure houses a complete recreation facility, including an NBA-size gymnasium; an older adult ministry complex, including respite care space for Alzheimer's patients; a nationally acclaimed infant and childcare center accommodating 200 children; additional space for youth and educational ministries; and an underground garage providing secure dropoff and pickup for our children and older adults, together with sixteen parking spaces for those with special needs.

Phase Two, the sanctuary: Our present sanctuary seats 1,100; the new sanctuary will seat approximately 2,400. I hasten to add that it will be a sanctuary, not an auditorium. Architecturally it will be similar to our present sanctuary, providing a warm intimate space in the classic Federalist style with a three-sided balcony like churches from this nation's early days. The building will reflect the traditional style, but will be boldly designed to take into account modern realities. We will worship in our present sanctuary until the day when our new sanctuary is complete. In order to construct the new sanctuary we will have to raze our present fellowship hall. The gymnasium in the life center will do double duty as a fellowship hall during the intervening time. Smaller structures on either side of the sanctuary will house our large and growing counseling center and a church parlor, a Session room, and support space for worship. Beneath the sanctuary will be a large, fully-equipped center for music and the arts.

Phase Three, the assembly hall: Our present sanctuary will be dismantled piece by piece, moved to the northeast corner of our block to be reconstructed as a fellowship hall with an adult conference and learning center above it.

Remember, we have a great history in downtown Orlando and we cherish it. Therefore, our sanctuary will be preserved but in a different form and with a different function. The present steeple will be removed and placed atop a tower structure 180-feet tall in the center of the block. The base of the tower is a small building housing a columbarium, where we shall secure the cremated remains of members of First Church who desire to have their final resting place on Church Street.

In a move back to the future we recapture the old concept of the church with the cemetery beside it and add a modern twist with the columbarium replacing the cemetery. (In addition, there will also be a place for the cremated remains of any who are homeless at the time of their death, allowing them the dignity of being remembered in the house of the Lord.) Phase Three, in a creative way, allows us to preserve our past as we move into our future.

Phase Four, retrofit and renovate existing educational buildings: The plan, conceived with such great flexibility, allows us in Phase Four to meet whatever requirements the church will be facing at that time. All of the structures on the block will then be connected by a colonnade, patterned after that created by Thomas Jefferson around the Great Lawn at the University of Virginia. The entire block will display both an architectural unity and a functional genius.

The next mountain for us to climb was the fund-raising campaign which, because of Operating Principle 1, had to be successful. There was no room for slippage. The first phase capital campaign had a goal of $7 million. We also made the decision that we would not be hiring professional fundraisers to conduct the campaign. Our own laypeople and staff would do the job, saving our church several hundred thousand dollars. We created the normal tools of communication such as reports, letters, brochures, and even a ten-minute video, all of which we placed in the hands of all our people.

Our purpose was to reawaken our people with regards to the details of the plan and to reenergize them toward making a financial commitment. However, before we went to the congregation as a whole with a call to financial commitment, we employed what is now lightheartedly referred to as the infamous "chicken salad strategy." In short here is what happened:

Trisha and I would invite forty members of our congregation to have lunch with us in the parlor of the church. Each of the forty had demonstrated leadership qualities and/or strong commitment in our church's life. An architectural model of the Master Plan project formed the centerpiece of the room. We were very careful with the time commitment we had asked of our guests, one hour. The food was on the tables and the eating began immediately after an opening greeting and a blessing. While the others were eating, I would describe the phases for the plan with particular emphasis on Phase One, using the architect's model as the visual aid.

By referring to the great story in Exodus 14, I reminded our people that when God's people, under the leadership of Moses, came to the edge of the Red Sea they were confronted with a fearsome challenge. The sea before them could not be bridged; behind them Pharaoh's army was in hot pursuit. They seemed to be stymied. Many of the people pleaded to go back to Egypt, back to the way things were. Even Moses could muster up no more courage than to say "Let's just hunker down and hang on." God then said, "Go forward." The moment they moved forward in faith and stuck their feet into the sea, the water parted and a glorious future opened before them. Holding that picture before our luncheon guests, I reminded our people we were much like the people of Israel. Some of us were no doubt wishing we could go back to the "good old days" when things were simple and uncomplicated. The thought certainly crossed my mind that it would be a lot easier for me personally to say, "Let's sit tight and maintain this ministry as it is." But I could not deny that God had called us to something greater, and none of us could deny that God had delivered confirming signs along the way indicating that we move ahead in faith.

Consequently, I called the people attending the lunch to take that step of faith. I had written a personal letter to each of our guests. In the letter was an actual gift figure that I hoped they would strive to meet. The figure had no scientific basis for its determination. My prayers for God's guidance coupled with my knowledge of each person produced the figure I placed in the letter. Here is a sample letter:

March 16, 1993
Dear_____
   I cannot thank you enough for allowing me the privilege of sharing with you what the future of our church holds. You are a vital part of this congregation. I know your commitment is deep and sincere. Therefore, I am convinced that together we can create here a church and a ministry that will be a blessing to us, to our children, and to all those who will come after us. Furthermore, I believe that a unique confluence of time and events in our city will allow us to exercise a transforming influence sufficient to keep our city a healthy, wholesome, hopeful place to live.
   In recent days, I have had a daily prayer time with your name before me, asking God to help us catch the vision and respond to His call. Because you are among the leaders in this church, I am asking you prayerfully, seriously, faithfully to consider making a substantial commitment to our campaign. My challenge to you is to consider a gift of $_____.
   That is a lot of money; I know that! But if you feel led by the Lord to rise to that great challenge, we will work overtime to enable you to fulfill that commitment in ways that are practical, satisfying, and of greatest benefit to you. Even if you feel that you cannot reach that goal at this time, I hope you will pray hard and think hard about making a significant commitment to the future of our church. We hope that you can fulfill that commitment in three years. Again, if that is not possible, then we shall be glad to work out a seven-year plan for you. Whatever your commitment may be, and however it

may be scheduled, what is important will be your personal involvement and leadership in making the dream come true for the work of Christ in this place.

You may rest assured that I will not be involved in any financial discussions, unless invited. All such discussions will be conducted with Ben McKenney or Kent Sterchi. However, I am available for personal discussion with you concerning the plan for our church and its ministry and for prayer.

We would like to receive your commitment by February 28, 1993. You may contact Mr. McKenney or Mr. Sterchi. If they do not hear from you, they will follow up by phone.

"We're Here For Life" is a catchy little phrase. I want it to be more than a phrase; I want it to be reality. With God's help and yours, it will be. Thank you again for considering this great challenge.

In Christ's love,

Howard Edington

Once again assuring people that their response to the letter would be handled by our staff in the business office and I would have no knowledge whether they responded or not, unless they desired to deal with me personally, I then sent them on their way to pray and to respond, if so led.

That is what happened at each lunch. These lunches were conducted nearly every working day for six weeks. Trisha and I hosted each lunch. The one-hour schedule was followed each day. Even the menu was the same chicken salad. We ate chicken salad every day for six weeks! Since the message was more important than the meal, we wanted to keep the meal tasty, but quick, easy, and light. Chicken salad was perfect. It freed us to pull out all the stops in delivering the message.

Did the "chicken salad strategy" work? Like gangbusters. We asked Kent Sterchi, our staff member who guided the campaign, why he thought the strategy proved so successful. Here are the reasons he shared:

1. The Master Plan was well-conceived and beautifully complete.
2. The operating principles addressed concerns and allayed fears.
3. Our people knew the depth of the commitment to downtown, and they desired to be a part of it.
4. The specific pledge amount placed before each potential donor raised their sights, sent them home with a grander vision, and allowed the Holy Spirit to move many to make sacrificial gifts.
5. People appreciated the colossal effort invested in the campaign by our lay leaders and staff.
6. The unveiling of the scale model of the church for the first time enabled the vision for this downtown block to "come to life," providing a visible image of the impact this church could have for Christ.

As a result, significant gifts from committed people began to come pouring in. And then something happened at which I still tremble with awe.

Late one afternoon I was sitting at my desk when the phone rang. The voice at the other end of the line said, "This is Craig Clayton. The members of the Clayton family have been having a family meeting and my father wants to speak to you."

While I waited for Malcolm Clayton to come to the phone, I could see with my mind's eye that great family: Malcolm Clayton, prominent commercial real estate developer, his wife Mary Damon, and their children and spouses: Ken and Joan Clayton, Bill and DeeDee Clayton Warren, Craig and Barbara Clayton, Phil and Carol Clayton Sealy, Brant and Yvonne Clayton, and Mark and Keli Clayton. Over the years, I have come to know and love them all so well.

Suddenly, that brief trip down memory lane was interrupted by Malcolm Clayton saying, "I'm calling to let you know that we as a family are committing ourselves to a seven-figure gift to the 'We're Here for Life Campaign.' " Tears of great joy sprang to my eyes and ran down my face. Wonder of wonders. God, working through Malcolm Clayton and his family, in one moment, in one phone call, in one sentence, had guaranteed the success of the campaign and the building of what would become known as the Clayton Life Center. Will I ever forget that phone call? Not as long as I live.

By the time we approached the full congregation with the financial campaign, two-thirds of the money had already been pledged. As I look back at that sentence and see how easily the words came, I am reminded that what actually happened came a lot harder than the words used to describe it. Not everyone was happy; not everyone responded with acclamation; not everyone agreed with the Master Plan or even with the need to have such a plan. Some refused to make a commitment. Some we lost to other churches. Not many, but a few. I would be a liar if I said it did not hurt to lose them. It did hurt, especially if they took a verbal shot as they left. But I learned a good lesson then: there is nothing worse than an unhappy camper in the Kingdom enterprise. I had to keep reminding myself that Jesus and his disciples went on a three-year camping trip. In their case, Judas was the unhappy camper. Jesus had to watch him go and I am sure it hurt. Yet looking back, in spite of the hurt, I am fairly certain that it was good for those unhappy souls to move on to another church family; I know it was good for us.

The rest of the congregation responded magnificently, the campaign was over-subscribed, and, before long, the rumble of heavy construction equipment punctuated the air at the heart of downtown Orlando. God and chicken salad proved to be a dynamic duo.

Former President Jimmy Carter in an interview in the *New York Times Magazine*, January 29, 1995, said this:

I have one life and one chance to make it count for something. I am free to choose what that something is, and the something I have chosen is my faith. Now, my faith goes beyond theology and religion and requires considerable work and effort. My faith demands—this is not optional—my faith demands that I do whatever I can, wherever I can, whenever I can, for as long as I can, with whatever I have to try to make a difference.[1]

With the Clayton family leading the way, the members of First Church committed in faith to do whatever we can, wherever we can, whenever we can, for as long as we can, with whatever we have, to try to make a difference for Jesus Christ at the center of our city.

One day the Lord will return to receive the return on his 120-year investment in the First Presbyterian Church of Orlando. Will we have multiplied what God has entrusted to us? I am content to let history answer the question.

CHAPTER IV

INITIATIVE:
The Miracle on Church Street

My guess is that Bill Owen would never have imagined that God would choose him to trigger a sequence of events that can only be termed "revolutionary."

Bill Owen's story is a great example of how one person's courage in living out his Christian beliefs enabled him to turn a transportation impact study, funded by the government, into a seedbed for the Christian faith. That seedbed planted with a variety of seeds has yielded very special, very needed "fruit" for the city of Orlando and for the churches in its downtown area. The story line is somewhat convoluted, but it is nonetheless fascinating. It all began when we at First Church wondered where we would park the cars.

Parking is probably the number one facility issue that all churches deal with at one time or another, but the challenge of solving parking problems downtown can be almost overwhelming. Possible solutions inevitably involve some combination of the following: large tracts of land which, if available at all, are very expensive; unattractive structures for which people are reluctant to spend ministry dollars; difficult, if not impossible, governmental regulations concerning traffic and environmental impacts; and safety concerns associated with people coming and going at other than normal business hours. Some churches in the face of these monstrous challenges simply opt out of the downtown area. However, for a church committed to remaining downtown, the challenge of finding a parking solution has to be met.

Bud Brakmann, who spearheaded our effort to solve the parking problem, described the parking available for our nearly 5,000-member congregation as "bits and pieces which have evolved over the years." Those bits and pieces he characterized as: convenient but very limited on-site parking; metered street parking, available only at night and on weekends; contract parking rented from an adjacent office building; and use of two nearby surface parking lots on Sunday on a shared and "as available" basis. The problems created by that patchwork approach to parking made it abundantly clear that if we were to undertake the Master Plan for developing our whole block, the program could not be viable without a permanent parking plan. Furthermore, without the building program, the growth and future of our downtown church was called into question.

With a gathering sense of urgency, we undertook a detailed examination of all available alternatives. Free parking spaces proved to be in short supply and were available only on nights and weekends. The possibility of renting or leasing parking spaces was ruled out as horrendously expensive. We even investigated the use of shuttle buses operating from remote areas, such as shopping centers on the outskirts of downtown. The shuttle bus scheme was soon rejected. While the buses can be rented, many buses would be required because the wait time at either end must be short and the heaviest usage would come in surges as services began and ended. Furthermore, it was a solution that would work only on Sunday morning, and the secret of success in a downtown church depends, in large degree, both on the quality and the quantity of its seven-day-a-week ministries. After eliminating those options, the only apparent solution was to build a parking garage on our property. The structure would be unattractive; it would be very expensive to build; it would consume the very limited property we possessed; and, even then, it would not be big enough to meet our full parking needs. No solution. Dead end. Brick wall. Nowhere to turn.

Could it be that parking problems would send our best laid plans "gang aft agley"?

While we were locked in a period of despair and indecision, as Bud Brakmann puts it, "An answer too perfect to be coincidence began to emerge." In casting about for solutions to our problem, we had chanced upon information that Orange County was running out of parking for its administration building located right across the street from us. They were investigating building a parking garage for which they had the property, but insufficient funding. Seizing what seemed to be our last hope, several members of our committee began conversations with our county officials to see if a mutually beneficial plan could be formulated. Discussions revolved around the possibility of using the property belonging to the county across the street from the church to construct a multilevel parking garage for use by both county and church. You can just imagine the kinds of problems that erupted out of those discussions. They were as numerous as bees circling a hive.

Then still another wrinkle. Orange County was building a courthouse on the north side of downtown. In order to complete that project, they needed a parcel of adjacent land that belonged to the city of Orlando. The two government entities engineered a swap. As a result, the city now owned the property across the street from our church. Suddenly three parties, Orange County, the city of Orlando, and First Church were engaged in the project. Conversations that could best be described as complex, suddenly became complicated to the extreme.

Enter Bill Owen. The city asked the Downtown Development Board to do a transportation study on the impact such a garage might have. Bill Owen was hired to do the study. He began by interviewing key people at First Church to determine what the long- and short-term parking needs might be. The more he delved into what was going on at our church the broader his study began to stretch. He began to realize that with automobile and pedestrian traffic, seven-day-a-week scheduled activities with long hours, 148 people working on site, the provision of numerous social services and the economic impact on the downtown core, First Church is a significant "industry." The impact the church was having on the city was largely going unnoticed by government planners and social agencies. Once Owen peeked into "the heart of the city" he was amazed at the variety, size, and quality of First Church's programming. He added into the mix the ministries of the other downtown churches and suddenly realized that he was breaking new ground. To complete his study, Owen pulled together representatives from the city, the county, the social service agencies, and the downtown churches. He began to describe what he had learned and suggested that all these folks should consider combining efforts to accomplish various priorities.

Seated in that meeting was Jim Cook, our associate minister for Congregational Life. His imagination is like gasoline, and that day Bill Owen tossed in a lighted match. Cook caught fire and in no time at all, he had our church establish the Downtown Church Council. It became a permanent association with representation from the city, the county, the churches, and the social agencies. Over succeeding months with regular meetings, solid relationships were formed and mutual problems in the downtown community were addressed and resolved. Jim Cook probably would defer the glory, but the reality is that for the first time the churches became "players" in the downtown arena. The work of the Downtown Church Council not only helped First Church, but it has also helped all the churches in downtown Orlando.

Now the stage was set for solving our parking problems, and we had no idea what drama would be unfolding on that stage. Each time the curtain rose on some new act, we were more surprised than before, and it became clear that some Higher Power was controlling the action. Negotiations with the city and the county now took place in the context of both deeper relationships and deeper understandings. We commissioned two of our church members, Peter Fox, an airline president, and Lee Chotas, a lawyer specializing in governmental relations, to head our negotiating team. They, together with their counterparts at the city of Orlando and Orange County, created an instrument unique in this country. "Revolutionary" is the way some have described it.

This is how the three partners arrived at such an unprecedented agreement. They altered the way governmental agencies viewed churches and their property. Historically the government viewed church property as nontax producing. Consequently, there has existed either subtle or overt hostility between the church and the government. That is no longer the case in Orlando. Because of the negotiations among the city, the county, and the church, the government agencies in our area look at First Church and, instead of saying, "What would that city block be worth on the tax rolls?" now they say, "If that church were not providing its services to the community, then the taxpayers would be forced to pay for such services." Peter Fox puts it in more businesslike terms:

When we started negotiating over the cost of impact fees, we asked the city to use a "program-based" methodology when calculating the fees rather than a "use-based" methodology. We basically told the city it was a disincentive for churches to stay downtown if they could not get credit for the social services they provide. The city has a history of finding ways to fund projects which may prove to be of ultimate benefit to the taxpayers. We simply asked that the church be understood in those terms, and we then demonstrated to the city the actual value to the taxpayers of the services the church provides.

Bolstered by this new way of looking at the value of the church to downtown, a true partnership among the city, the county, and the church was formed. Out of the partnership there emerged a plan crafted to meet the unique parking requirements of the three partners at minimum cost to each.

The plan called for a multilevel parking garage, with a capacity of 900 cars to be constructed on the property adjacent to the county administration building and across the street from the church. Each partner, investing one-third of the total cost, receives 300 of the parking spaces for use twenty-four hours a day, seven days a week. However, because the county's needs occur only during daytime working hours, their 300 spaces would be made available for church use in the evenings and on weekends. Furthermore, on Sundays, the 300 spaces that belonged to the city would also be made available to the church. Add it up: that gave the church 900 parking spaces at the time when we need them the most. Thus, the church's peak time and long-term parking demands would be met. The city, which builds and operates all the downtown parking garages would operate this one, thus lowering the cost of operation and maintenance, plus providing the advantage of being part of the city's security system.

In hindsight, it is obvious that could we have had any parking solution we desired, this would be it. But we could never have arrived at this solution on our own. In our present national climate, when the issues of church and state relations are fraught with such controversy, and confounded by issues of religious pluralism, who would dare to think about a shared county-city-church facility on government property located directly across from the church? Well, the reality is, we didn't think about it. After two years of diligent work that exhausted every reasonable solution, this program "dropped out of heaven," not just figuratively but literally. True, we were there at the right time with the necessary background to appreciate it, but we cannot and do not take credit for it.

Still, the story unfolds. The partnership now firmly established between the church, the local government, and the business communities is expressed in a number of ways.

Exhibit A: Our church, working in partnership with an agency of the city, the Center for Drug Free Living, now conducts a midnight basketball program in our gymnasium to take young people off the streets where drugs can be found and place them in a wholesome environment where a different style of life can be found. The lights in the gymnasium of the Clayton Life Center burn all during the night now as kids are being pulled away from the lure of mischief and crime in the society in which we live.

Exhibit B: Our church works in partnership with the city zoning and planning boards to keep the downtown wholesome and safe. We operate on the principle of quid pro quo. It does mean that the church makes minor compromises in order to preserve major principles. For example, there is an ordinance in our city making it illegal for a business establishment to serve alcoholic beverages within 1,000 feet of church property. On several occasions we have yielded to the city's request to establish upscale restaurants that serve wine within 1,000 feet of the church. That concession gives us the leverage to prevent the establishment of night clubs that serve hard liquor, exploit women, operate at all hours, and foster a drug culture. We cooperate with the city in areas where no major harm will be done in order to have the city's cooperation in keeping the area around the church safe and secure.

Exhibit C: Several blocks east of the church is Howard Middle School. The student body is largely African American, many of them living several blocks west of the church. Every day after school those kids cross our church property as they are headed home. For many of them, there is no one waiting for them at home. The parents have to work, so the children are on the street and there too easily they get into trouble. Working in partnership with the school, we are stopping those kids at our block. And after school, we offer them tutorial programs to strengthen them academically, recreational activities, instruction in music and the arts, and the opportunity, if they choose, to engage in Bible studies and spiritual growth groups. It is our conviction that we will make a difference in these children's lives and in turn they will make a difference in our church and our city.

Exhibit D: The headline in *The Orlando Sentinel* read, "Church Expansion Plan Has City's Blessing." The article under that headline went on to describe how the Master Plan for the development for the block on which we sit has gained not just the approval but the enthusiastic endorsement of city officials. What is happening at First Church city officials say is, "A sign that downtown is recovering from the real estate slump of the late 1980s and early 1990s." How rare that kind of article is in our country's newspapers today, but it is clear from the article that the city regards the ministry of the church as being important enough to support and to encourage.

Recognition of this unique partnership led Glenda Hood, the mayor of Orlando, to say:

We are blessed in downtown Orlando to have a balance of businesses, residential communities, entertainment establishments, and religious organizations. All are encouraged to work together as a community. Our churches are important from a spiritual aspect as well as the development of programs for inner city youth, seniors, and other areas of education. When so many cities are losing religious institutions in the inner city, Orlando is successfully supporting this vitally important component.

Surely it is obvious that the partnership forged in the downtown community is paying significant dividends already. It hasn't all been easy. Lyle Schaller, in his book, *Center City Churches*, writes:

Doing ministry in the large central city, may be fun, but it is neither simple nor easy. It is challenging, and meeting challenges can produce immense satisfaction, but that effort also can result in a string of frustrating experiences.[1]

To be sure, at First Church we have had our frustrating experiences, but the fun far outweighs the frustration.

I have become convinced that what has happened here in Orlando, while unique in this country so far as we can determine, nevertheless can be translated to other churches and other cities. We have learned some critical lessons and plowed some new ground. Those lessons are available and they will make the plowing of the ground where you are much easier. The lessons are:

1. The church has to take the initiative in helping local officials understand the value, yes, even the dollar value, of what the church is doing in the community.

2. Constitutional issues, while complex and even vexing, are not insurmountable. Extensive negotiations, in our case, resulted in a formal contract between the city of Orlando, Orange County, and First Church, and that contract has been ruled constitutional.

3. The church must demonstrate a clear commitment to the health and welfare of the downtown community and must be willing to back up this commitment with action.

4. In any joint developments, use of property owned by government or private individual is preferable to church property particularly if the church has denominational ties. In such instances, the issue of land ownership becomes hopelessly complex. The church is better at bringing to the partnership financial and human resources.

5. The church must be creative in developing plans and programs that are mutually beneficial to the local government and business communities in downtown. Such a strategy wins the devotion and support of those people for the church's existence.

Robert Borgwardt, writing in the volume titled, *Center City Churches*, declares that:

The most common response of the downtown church during the second half of the twentieth century was to grow older and smaller. A second was to relocate to a more hospitable setting. A third, but far less common response to the turmoil, was to accept the role of a regional church and expand the variety of ministries.[2]

First Church not only has taken the less common response of becoming a regional church and expanding the variety of its ministries, but also has pursued the unique response of changing the whole character of the relationship that exists between the downtown church and the city surrounding it.

Can you believe it? This revolutionary idea and everything emerging from it, was triggered one day when a man named Bill Owen, a professional consultant to city government, who also happened to be Christian, was hired to conduct a transportation impact study in downtown Orlando.

We call it "The Miracle on Church Street."

CHAPTER V

INTEGRITY:
The Covenant Concept for Staff

Jesus, CEO. In a book under that improbable title, Laurie Beth Jones reminds us that Jesus called a staff. He built a team. He recognized that the effectiveness of his own ministry would be determined by those who shared the ministry with him. As Jones puts it:

In His final recorded prayer on earth, Jesus said, "These people were your gift to me": He taught them and He trained them, but His joy did not come from the end result. It came from the process and from their companionship. Your staff members may or may not execute the plans that you have so brilliantly set before them. However, you must never forget that these people are, most of all, *Someone's* greatest gifts to you. Enjoy them. Cherish them. Defend them. Relish them. To shepherd a flock of butterflies one must stand there in delight. Jesus saw them as God's gift to Him.[1]

Laurie Beth Jones articulates and analyzes Jesus' extraordinary leadership and management skills. Then in a step every bit as improbable as the title of her book, she applies his techniques to corporate America. I would contend that the call to visionary leadership that she propounds also can be applied to the downtown church, particularly when it comes to building a staff.

Experience in tackling the downtown challenges has taught us that when it comes to staff, *people count more than positions, and faith counts more than function.* I have sought to capture our approach by using the word "integrity." Obviously I am referring in part to the quality of life lived by the ministerial staff, but it is much more than that as well. At First Church we strive to create an integrity to the ministry of the whole; that is, a concept or a style of ministry that is clear, transparent, obvious to everyone who beholds it, nothing hidden, nothing held back. We label it "the covenant concept." Ministers called to our staff engage in a covenant structured to make us committed and effective in our work and loyal and accountable to one another. We stumbled into the covenant concept accidentally, or more accurately, providentially.

When I arrived in Orlando in June of 1982, I inherited a staff that appeared to be virtually complete. This was both an optical and a spiritual illusion. Within days of my arrival it was as if the door of the church had become a revolving door. One of the ministers made an appointment with me to say that during the vacancy she had engaged in conversations with several other churches and was now ready to accept a call to a church in Texas. She was married to the director of our counseling center, and when she left, he left. Not long thereafter, the business administrator, an ordained minister, approached me with the news that he no longer wished to function in administration and wanted responsibilities in the area of pastoral care. Since at that time the pastoral care position was filled, he opted to seek a call elsewhere. Reeling under these unexpected developments, I next had to face directives from the Session regarding two other staff members. After a process of review that had begun before I arrived, our elders reached the decision that these staff members did not mesh with the mission of our church and, therefore, would have to be replaced. Then came the final straw which, never mind the camel, nearly broke my back. Six months after my arrival, the lead associate dropped a gauntlet-like challenge in the form of a letter to me that he left on my desk and then departed for a week of vacation. In the letter he declared that it had been his desire to be the senior minister at First Church and, in his view, had it not been for a "quirky" policy in the Presbyterian *Book of*

Order prohibiting associates from succeeding their senior ministers, the position would have been his. Therefore, he was demanding that the preaching responsibilities be split fifty-fifty. My astonishment was exceeded only by the absurdity of it all. I summoned members of the Session and members comprising the search committee that had called me to Orlando. To them I put the simple question, "Is there any justification for this request?" Their unanimous, unequivocal response: "No. He must go."

Nightmare on Church Street. Within a year of my arrival, I found myself serving a struggling church with no staff. The strain and stress of it all took its toll on me physically. I developed ulcerative colitis, hardly an exotic condition. The spiritual toll was equally devastating. I questioned my abilities to deal with the problems we faced. I even began to wonder if those who had counseled me against tackling the downtown church had been right all along. Granddaddy's words reached out and caught hold of my soul again: "Things will change and disappear, but Jesus never will. When nothing else seems certain, Jesus is." I held on to those words for dear life.

The next several months proved to be a turning point both for me and for the church. Following normal Presbyterian procedure, we elected five search committees—*five*—to secure people to fill the vacant positions. I was meeting with a different committee every night, and none of the committees knew what the others were doing; I was the only common thread. In the meantime, the work of the church was spinning aimlessly, fruitlessly like automobile tires in a quagmire.

Blessedly, thankfully, and not a moment too soon, the elders on our Session recognized that what was transpiring probably would kill me and perhaps even kill the church. They called a special meeting to pray and diligently seek the guiding hand of God. I look back to that meeting as a watershed moment. After an extended season of prayer, one of the elders, a giant of a man spiritually, and in my own heart's affection, took to his feet with a stirring word:

We are viewing what is happening as an obstacle when I believe that God views it as an opportunity. We are seeing all the staff vacancies as a brake upon our work, but I believe God sees it as a blank slate upon which we can create something new. Never before in the modern history of this church have we had the opportunity to build the staff from scratch. Let's dare to do something we have never done before.

The Session then took the unprecedented step of abolishing the five existent committees and creating one committee with one job to do: build a staff. The Session decreed (and it became a guiding principle to which we cling even now) that instead of searching for people to fill certain positions, we would search for the most committed, multitalented, multigifted people we could find and structure positions in which they could thrive. With that action the seeds of new life were planted in a struggling downtown church and in a weary preacher's soul. The healing had begun.

By the fall of 1983, the search committee had secured John Tolson, Jim McNaull, and Tino Ballesteros, three monumentally gifted men, and the engine of the old church began to fire up again. As each of the four of us began charging out in the directions of our individual gifts and abilities, it quickly became apparent that some adhesive force would be required to hold us together and to keep us on course. The covenant was born. The covenant in its present form looks like this:

A COVENANT

Preamble

This covenant shall govern our relationship to one another as ministers of the First Presbyterian Church of Orlando, Florida. Living and working together under the terms of this agreement will enable us to become all that God intends us to be in calling us to His service in this church. We subscribe to the covenant and we encourage the congregation to support us as we seek to live by it. Under the leadership of God's Spirit, the congregation may wish to consider similar covenant relationships for their own lives.

Accountability

The called leaders shall commit themselves not simply to individual spiritual growth, but to spiritual development as a team. That is, they shall structure the means regularly to pray together, to study together, to worship together, to love one another, to stretch and challenge each other, to sharpen and refine one another's gifts devoting time to contemplation as well as action. They shall, by the quality and consistency of their walk with the Lord and with each other, demonstrate what it means to live and to love and to serve "in Christ." The called leaders shall strive for "excellence unto the Lord" and become accountable to one another in strength and in weakness. When, for any reason, it seems that God is directing any one of us out of a leadership calling here, our covenant is that the exploration of the change, and the change if it takes place, be an experience of Christian love and a delicate care to avoid damage to the one who goes and the ones who remain.

Loyalty

The called leaders shall be bound to one another not by blind loyalty but by Christ's kind of loyalty. That is, differences among team members shall be prayed, worked, and fought through behind closed doors. The discipline of confidentiality will be honored among team members. Once team decisions are reached to which all can subscribe, then a unified front can and shall be presented to the congregation. In addition, the commitment to loyally support one another, not only in terms of ministry needs but also in terms of personal needs, is essential. Team members shall be utterly supportive of one another in the presence of other people. For example, if someone shares with one minister a negative and critical comment concerning another member of the team, the immediate response shall be, "That person is my friend and my colleague. If we have a problem then we shall go together to that person to discuss the matter" (Matt. 5:22).

Flexibility

The called leaders shall be willing to apply their individual gifts to any aspect of the church's ministry as circumstances may warrant. That is, if one team member involved in one dimension of the church's work should require the working support of other team members, the team shall respond, willingly and eagerly, as quickly as possible. In addition, the team shall bring to bear the full force of its abilities upon matters of a top-priority or emergency nature. Also, the team members shall be flexible enough to coordinate personal ministry and time-away schedules to serve the best interests of the church and the team. While each team member is directly responsible for his or her department, all members are responsible for all aspects of the church's ministry. Therefore, each should be willing to use any or all of his or her talents to assist and build up every area of the church and the team.

With staff changes over the years and incoming staff people bringing new insights to the process, the covenant has changed in some of its details, but the essence has remained the same. The nature of the covenant allows us to make affirmations for staffing the downtown church:

❏ **We affirm that the only significant criteria for staff are character, Christian commitment, and competence.** Those criteria, lifted straight from page 93 of Lyle Schaller's *The Seven-Day-a-Week Church*, govern our pursuit of individuals to join us in this ministry. Borrowing the term from Laurie Beth Jones, we are looking for *butterfly* people, not *caterpillar* people. We are looking for the strongest, most committed, most gifted people we can find. We are not looking for people to do a job; we are looking for people who want to bring their manifold gifts to partner with us in the kingdom enterprise. Lou Holtz, the great football coach at Notre Dame, when asked how he approached recruiting players, replied, "I never recruit players to fill particular positions on the team. Instead, I recruit the best all-around athletes we can find and then build the team around their abilities." What Lou Holtz does at Notre Dame we do at First Church. Three things do matter to us: character, commitment to Christ, and competence. Does the person's manner and quality of life reflect the values espoused on the pages of the New Testament? Does the person's commitment to Jesus Christ reflect the unreserved, unashamed, unequivocal devotion to Christ that our church proclaims? Does the person have the ability to function effectively in all facets of the church's ministry? A person passing that threefold test is sure to be a productive and complementary partner in our work. When I look at the members of our administrative staff, I thrill to the knowledge that each of them is perfectly capable of filling my own position. They soar like butterflies, and to shepherd a bunch of butterflies one must simply stand there in delight.

❑ **We affirm that all administrative staffers shall be engaged in all aspects of the church's ministry.** We do have titles and we affix titles to office doors so that people who come to the church can find the particular individual they are seeking. But the reality is that the title hanging on the door is meaningless in terms of the ministry of the church. One reason is that the ministry of the downtown church is so dynamic and in such constant flux that we have concluded a tight hierarchical system cannot work in that setting. Therefore, in our system I function as first among equals, that is to say, our intent is to arrive at decision by consensus. If, on those rarest of occasions, we cannot reach a consensus and a decision has to be made, then I will make it. Let me repeat: that happens on only the rarest of occasions. The consensus style gives us the flexibility we need to confront the ever-changing challenges of downtown.

Another reason the staff has to be engaged in every dimension of the church's ministry is to ensure that the ministry of First Church belongs not to Howard Edington but to the whole staff. My role approximates Lyle Schaller's winsome description:

The senior minister seeks entrepreneurial personalities who are motivational leaders for the staff, enjoys watching the growing competition among them, laughs at the problems this sometimes creates, helps raise the money necessary to fund this giant circus, and adjourns staff meetings with the admonition, "Sic em!"[2]

At First Church everybody on the staff is equally vested, that is, vested at the point of their gifts. For example, Ted Pierce has a superb gift in dealing with children and youth. The title hanging on his door is "Minister of Education and Program." He does oversee our church's entire educational ministry, but he is also involved in evangelism, pastoral care, worship, and administration. He functions across the whole range of our church's life, but his involvement in those areas comes primarily at the point of his pronounced gifts with children and youth. Ted Pierce is typical. All of us are engaged in all aspects of the church's ministry.

❑ **We affirm that each staffer must "go deep" in at least one area of the church's life.** Here is the other side to the coin. While all of us on the ministerial staff are equally engaged in every aspect of the church's work, each of us also is expected to pour significant ability and energy into one or more dimensions of our ministry. That's what we mean by the phrase "go deep." We "go deep" in the area of our most pronounced gifts. For example, David Baker's gift for singles, Roy Riviere's gift for adult education, and Ben McKenney's gift for administration determine the areas where those individuals "go deep" in our ministry. I "go deep" in the preaching ministry. Put it another way. It is not accurate in reality, but we want the people of First Church to regard individuals on the staff as being indispensable to particular areas of our church's work. We want, for example, our people to believe in their hearts that if we did not have Bill Duckworth as minister of Pastoral Care, the church might fall apart. Now, of course, that is not true. If Bill Duckworth, or any of us for that matter, were to leave tomorrow, the Lord would simply lead us to someone else. But we do not want the people to feel that. We want them to feel that if we were to lose that person we would not make it. I still chuckle with great satisfaction at a letter I received a couple of years ago signed by the members of our Board of Deacons. The Board of Deacons provides our hands-on ministry of caring and serving. It is in those areas and with that board that Bill Duckworth has "gone deep" in his ministry among us. The letter read: "Dear Howard, we are aware of the fact that we could find another senior minister should that be necessary, but you need to do whatever is necessary for us to keep from losing Bill Duckworth." The letter was signed by each deacon. They got it. Yes, indeed, they got it! We want our people to feel that every individual on our administrative staff is so crucial to some facet of our work that we simply could not get along without them.

❑ **We affirm that nobody wins until we all do.** Laurie Beth Jones again:

I thought about Jesus choosing to tell about the shepherd who cannot rest as long as even one sheep is still missing, despite the ninety-nine of them which aren't . . . about a father who is waiting on the road, watching for his lost son to come home, even though he has one son who is serving him ably and well . . . about a king holding a banquet, who will not start serving dinner until every place is filled at the Great Table . . . and I wonder what this world would be like if we played by that rule: that nobody wins until we all do.[3]

In other words, the covenant concept demands a deep and genuine loyalty, each of us to the others. We cannot have harmful competing elements on the staff. We cannot sanction the building of little kingdoms and constituencies internally. We cannot tolerate members of the congregation practicing "triangulation," that is, playing one staff member over against another. Our commitment to loyalty is the adhesive that holds us together. We are committed to the premise that nobody wins until we all do.

❑ **We affirm that we are ultimately accountable to God and immediately accountable to one another.** Laurie Beth Jones one more time:

Accountability is the key factor in management because it is the cornerstone of empowerment and personal growth. If no one is accountable for a project, no one gets to grow through the experience of it. Accountability has nothing to do with blame. It has everything to do with individual and corporate growth. Jesus said, "Whatever you ask for will be done. Whatever you loose on earth will be loosed in heaven. Whatever you bind up will be bound." Jesus held people accountable.[4]

Because the binding nature of our covenant makes us accountable to one another, we do not have to manufacture artificial enthusiasm for the work of the church. All the bases of our shared ministry must be covered, and we are the ones who will do the covering. No one ever needs to ask, "Who is going to be responsible for this particular program or function?" We all are. No one ever dares to say, "That is not in my job description." The whole ministry of the church belongs to each of us and to all of us. We are accountable to Jesus and we are accountable to one another.

The covenant concept fosters a genuine team spirit which, by their own acclamation, is observable to members of our congregation. That is what we mean by the use of the word "integrity." It refers to a ministry in which all of us are equally and openly and honestly engaged. What works for us can work for you.

CHAPTER VI

INVOLVEMENT:
All Things to All People: 24–7–365

My friend Toasy Martin, who claims to stay in touch with whatever is the current rage, tells me that "24-7-365" is now a popular slang expression. It means *all the time*, "24 hours a day, 7 days a week, 365 days a year." Therefore, one can say, "I'm working 24-7-365" or "I'm having fun 24-7-365."

Lyle Schaller wrote a marvelous book entitled *The Seven-Day-a-Week Church*. Our church is determined to force him to write a sequel, *The 24-Hour-a-Day Church*. At First Church, in the not too distant future, we shall declare, "Our church is 24-7-365." In other words, it will be functioning around the clock and around the calendar.

In *FaithQuotes* Leonard Sweet quotes Leith Anderson, who is pastor of the forward-looking Wooddale Church in Minneapolis, as he paints a descriptive picture:

The primary entry into church is not one big Sunday morning door, but a plethora of little doors that open seven days a week. Churches must be less and less of a Sunday morning phenomenon, and more of a seven mornings and seven afternoons and seven evenings every week phenomenon.[1]

What about seven middle-of-the-nights? Not as farfetched as you might think. All the time, 24-7-365, is soon to come to First Church. We are not far from that now!

For you to understand how our church can operate 24-7-365 you need to understand our philosophy of ministry, our approach to programming, and our utilization of facilities. Like the layers of an onion, I peel them away one at a time.

Philosophy of Ministry

People are forever saying to me, "You can't be all things to all people. You need to find a specific area of ministry, concentrate on that, and do it well." Not downtown. Downtown it is even more pronounced that you have to be "all things to all people." Furthermore, you not only have to be all things, you also have to do all things, and you have to do them well. Why? Because every one of those 5,000 people at First Church goes to great inconvenience to get to church. They travel long distances; they pass by who knows how many other churches; and they scramble to find a parking place. Therefore, the only way we can make it downtown is to provide such a variety of ministries, functioning at such a level of competence, that people will suffer any inconvenience to be involved. There are, at present, 152 different ministries that originate from the base of First Church. When we say we are determined to be all things to all people, we are not simply playing word games. The effort to develop an over-arching philosophy for our smorgasbord of ministries prompted certain questions:

1. What plans do we have to develop our people spiritually, in ways that equip them to proceed competently into the twenty-first century as salt and light to the world?

2. As we chart a path and develop needed facilities, how will the staff and lay leaders of First Church go forward together to help people along the spiritual path?

3. Does our church have a comprehensive plan to provide our people with spiritual education that is developmental in scope, progressive in vision, and inclusive of all ages?

Wrestling with those questions led us to establish twin emphases for all our ministries: contemplation and action. The true Christian life, based on the truest Christian life of all—the life of Jesus—strikes a balance between the inreach of contemplation and the outreach of action. Jesus threw himself, without reserve, into the activity of his ministry. But, he could do that only because, occasionally, he pulled apart to be with God. We understand *contemplation* to be acts of reflection, accomplished in quietness and solitude, or in active communion with others, where one searches one's heart for the still, small voice of God by way of prayer, Christian meditation, fasting, quiet days, journaling, and artistic expression. We understand *action* to be replicating Christ's ministry of preaching, teaching and healing through public and private worship, disciplined study of the Scripture and the beliefs of the church, caring for one another in a community of Christian relationships, and serving God through tangible expressions of love for people and the world. Every ministry flowing out of our church must now demonstrate both a *contemplative* side and an *active* side. So critical do we regard this strategy and this philosophy of ministry that we have called David Baker to our staff as director of Spiritual Formation. In a world that is becoming increasingly apathetic, if not hostile, to the Christian faith, Christians need to be tough-minded. In a world where human need is mountainous in proportion, Christians must be tenderhearted. First Church is bent on producing tough-minded, tenderhearted Christians who, because of their own personal transformation in Christ, are equipped to transform our society and our world for Christ.

Furthermore, an ancillary part of that philosophy is an emphasis on centralizing. Virtually everything we do is designed to bring people downtown at some point in the week, and preferably more than just once during the week. We believe that our only hope is to draw people to that base on Church Street, to engage them in significant spiritual growth opportunities *there*, to allow them to experience the dynamic of the spirit that exists *there*; only then will they be moved to return. We do not have the luxury of appealing to a certain kind of person or a certain niche of ministry. We have no choice but to try to lure people downtown. Therefore, we do not engage in sending satellites of our ministry to outlying areas. Our ministry is centralized, pulling our people to Church Street. We have to be all things to all people.

Approach to Programming

All of our church's programming falls under the rubric of contemplation/action. But in its practical application our programming places primary emphasis on *the church family*. The term does not simply denote the nuclear families who are a part of our church. Like it or not, the traditional family unit is no longer as predominant as it once was. Now, broken families, blended families, single-parent families, dysfunctional families, and single adults living as a one-person family are the reality of our age. Once upon a time, a person's basic needs in life were met primarily through a nuclear family or an extended family. This is no longer true. Consequently, our church delivers the message to all who come to us regardless of their circumstances: "We are your family." Most of the programs and activities we offer are designed to enhance the sense of belonging to a family.

We also engage in *symbiotic* programming. If you visit Disney World, as most everyone does sooner or later, check out the Land Pavilion at EPCOT Center. The pavilion features a remarkable film entitled *Symbiosis*. The movie vividly portrays how some elements of creation exist in a symbiotic relationship. That is, two organisms supporting each other. A parasitic relationship is one organism living off of another. But in symbiosis, two organisms live off of each other. For example, in Africa the rhinoceros always has a little bird riding on his back. The bird is called the tick bird. The two creatures actually support each other. The rhinoceros with big strong hooves plows up the ground unearthing insects that the tick bird then eats. That is what the rhinoceros does for the tick bird. The thick hide of the rhinoceros has deep folds and crevices within it. Parasites can imbed themselves in its folds and create severe problems for the rhino. The tick bird riding about on the rhino's back forages down in those folds. That is what the bird does for the rhino. Symbiosis: two organisms living off of each other.

Transfer that principle from the wilds of Africa to downtown Orlando. Our programs never function in a vacuum, never stand in isolation. We must plan carefully so that the programs support and feed off of one another. Why? Simply because of the great distances that people have to travel to get to us. For example, Wednesday Night R and R. Born out of the mind and heart of Beth Edington Hewitt who does double duty as my daughter and as the director of Children's Ministry, R and R has four basic themes and three tracks. The themes are:

Relax and recreate! By using our dynamic recreation center and equipment, our people have an opportunity to build relationships through wholesome play and team activities.

Rejoice and rehearse! We provide an informal worship service together with age-graded choir rehearsals and participation in drama and other creative arts.

Refresh and revive! Mealtime is structured to create a sense of church family with all eating together in a nurturing environment.

Renew and recharge! This is the time for small group experiences, intensive Bible study classes, arts and crafts, and mission activities.

Those four themes have three tracks: children, youth, and adults. Each track experiences all four themes every Wednesday. Here you have symbiotic programming at its best. Think of the problem created by an isolated program for children. Parents would bring their children downtown, usually at some distance. There would not be enough time to drop the children off at the beginning of the program, drive all the way home, and then return to pick them up at the end of the program. We learned quickly that if we have an activity for children, we must have activities for adults at the same time, and vice versa.

Another example: In our physical facility we have placed our Infant/Child Care Center adjacent to our Adult Activity Center. We did that for a good reason: symbiosis. Our older adults go into the rooms where the babies are and spend hours holding the babies in their arms and rocking them to sleep. Babies need to be loved and older adults love to be needed. We have a "gardening patio" where older adults and children work together planting seeds, growing plants, pulling weeds, sharing life. Symbiosis. Every program has to support and feed off of every other program. Symbiosis.

In addition to providing the basic programs and activities you would find in most churches, you will find a heavy emphasis placed on what we call *needs-based ministry*. There are dozens and dozens of such ministries at First Church, but let me give you just a sampling.

Gathering of Men

Long before Promise Keepers was ever a gleam in Bill McCartney's eye, John Tolson, our minister of Outreach, with his extraordinary gift for communicating the gospel, developed a ministry to men that began at First Church and has spread across the country. Leonard Sweet writing in *FaithQuakes* declares:

The best way to reach people . . . is show them that you care about their work. This is where people spend their lives. Since this is where people make their "living," this ought to be where the church shows people how to truly live. The gospel changes bad habits of living and bad habits of thinking into successful patterns of whole-life living and thinking. It transposes one's work into a divine key. . . . For men, (i.e., male-order living), who have gone from bar crawls in college to boardroom brawls in business, this often means helping them see how some lost meanings of machoness and success are well lost.[2]

The ministry of The Gathering confronts men with the claims of Christ in their lives, draws them into fellowship with other Christian men, and strengthens their witness for Christ in their vocational pursuits. One of the weekly activities of The Gathering is a luncheon in our Lee Fellowship Hall where 350 to 400 men have a light lunch and a heavy Bible study. My office window is immediately across the church courtyard from the entrance to Lee Fellowship Hall. Every week, thirty minutes or so after The Gathering lunch, I can look out of my window and see the courtyard filled with groups or pairs of men talking together. They are making business deals, discussing sports, and sharing burdens. Nothing unusual about that, except in this instance, it is being done in the context of the faith. We could fill a book with the stories of how men, energized in their faith by The Gathering, have made a difference in the business and professional community of Orlando. (While many of the men in The Gathering come from other churches, no minister from any other church has ever objected to the work of The Gathering. If you are a preacher, that tells you all you need to know about the quality of this ministry.)

Open Hearts

Divorce affects all levels of society, but without exception the innocent victims are the children involved. During a separation or divorce, most parents' are facing such difficulties within themselves they are unable to provide the emotional support a child needs. The children are confused, frightened and, much worse, prone to think they are the cause of their parents breakup. Faced with that reality, Alene Baker, with a voice soft as a gently flowing stream and a heart as big as all outdoors, took it upon herself to meet the spiritual and emotional needs of children in shattered families. We call it Open Hearts. There is no other ministry like it in the city of Orlando and consequently children come, not only from our own church, but also by referral from other churches, the public schools, and social service agencies. Amazingly enough, it is staffed by people who, like Alene Baker, are volunteers. They have developed their own curriculum and their own style of ministry. Furthermore, they undergo significant training. They deal with subjects such as anger, self-blame, emotional stress, and feelings of self-worth from the perspective of faith. The program is not designed to professionally counsel children, but to offer them a safe, loving place to share their hurts and concerns with other children going through the same trials, and to draw strength and hope from adult Christians who love them unconditionally. Alene Baker can speak for herself:

When I started with Open Hearts I knew immediately this was where the Lord wanted me to be. To see these little people with broken hearts come into a loving Christian atmosphere each week, begin to let the barriers down, and start a healing process is truly a joy to experience. Sometimes when we look at the mountain of problems our young people face today, it seems insurmountable. By taking small steps in ministries, such as Open Hearts, we can possibly change the direction and hope of a young person's life. We have to start somewhere, and I love being a part of a church family that cares enough to support such a ministry.

Missionary Computer Fellowship

One day George Wilson walked into my office and sat down. George was an engineering supervisor at one of the nation's leading defense contractors. He said, "Preacher, I listen to you preach Jesus Sunday after Sunday. I've spent my whole life building bombs to destroy people. For the sake of Jesus I want to spend the rest of my life trying to help people. Let me tell you what I have in mind." He began to tell me. I did not understand the first word he said. He was using language from the field of technology, and I did not have a clue as to what the words meant. In fact, the more he talked the more bewildered I became. Finally, he uttered a word I did understand; the word was "missions." I interrupted him, "George, is what you are talking about going to involve our church's work in missions?" His face brightened. "Yes, it has to do with missions. Especially with medical missions."

Now it was the time for my face to brighten up. "George, as God's providence would have it, Dr. David Seel, one of our Presbyterian missionaries in Korea, will be visiting our church next week. Perhaps you can make him understand what you are talking about, because it is completely beyond me."

The next week, I took Dave Seel and George Wilson out to lunch, sat there for two hours, and never understood a word either one of them said! But they understood each other, and what was born that day is nothing short of incredible. Begun as one man's idea in obedience to Christ, the Missionary Computer Fellowship now occupies the basement of one of our buildings. The ministry is staffed by a group of twenty-five people who work eight hours a day as volunteers. Most of them have taken early retirement from the high tech world. They are all technological wizards. They work down there in the basement, full time, with no pay, just because they love the Lord. They have an assembly line. They take old computers donated by individuals and companies moving to the next generation of PC's. On the assembly line they re-manufacture those computers to make them "jungle proof." They make the hardware capable of functioning in any climatological setting. Working through denominations and mission-sending agencies, we bring missionaries to spend at least a week in our basement. Usually they live with members of our church for that time. The volunteers of Missionary Computer Fellowship find out what a particular missionary's needs are; develop software appropriate for their ministry; train them in the use of both the software and the hardware; and then send them with their new equipment back into the field. Over the last two years, we have had more than one thousand missionaries go through the basement of First Church, better able to do the work of Christ on the mission field. All because one day George Wilson said, "I want to do something for the Lord."

Special Needs Council

Bubbling up from the spiritual ferment of this great congregation, this council functioned for six months with lay leaders before there was any staff involvement at all. How did it happen? Parents who had children with special needs or disabilities began to talk with one another about meeting the spiritual needs of their children. Other people in the congregation, professionals with expertise or experience in these areas, entered the conversations. The Lord was there, too. They began by addressing the physical barriers presented by First Church. Their ideas flowed into the development of the Master Plan, and, as a result, within the foreseeable future no physical barrier will deny access to any person wishing to take part in the programs and activities of First Church. Yet a more subtle, but perhaps more painful problem, still remained. Once those persons arrived on our campus physically, how would they be welcomed and integrated into the program ministries? The council began an educational program starting with staff and moving to the hundreds of volunteers who lead our programs and activities. Here are some results:

- Our Infant/Child Care Center is the only center in Orlando to take children who are on heart monitors. We also take "snow babies," children born to cocaine-addicted mothers. And we are learning that in an atmosphere of Christian love these children can achieve greater development than was previously thought possible.

- Our Life Center includes a medical clinic staffed by volunteer doctors and nurses from the congregation, meeting the basic medical needs of children in the Infant/Child Care Center and the homeless.
- The rooms of our church nurseries are all staffed with volunteers and must include one registered nurse, trained to provide special care for children facing difficult challenges.
- Sharon Todd, affected by cerebral palsy and operating from a wheelchair, serves on our youth ministry staff. By her own design, the focal point of her ministry is young people on the fringes of the group. Once you have been touched by her radiant spirit, you feel on the fringe no more.
- Our Sunday school teachers and classes are now able to handle any child with a special need. At a recent Sunday school teacher training session, Sonja Schoonmaker, shared with the group her profound gratitude at what the Sunday school experience had meant to her daughter Alycia, who has cerebral palsy and is mentally delayed. Sunday school has become one of Alycia's great joys in life. Then one of Alycia's teachers, Federico Jové, stood to share how Alycia's presence in the class had made such a difference in his life. A room full of Sunday school teachers, suddenly brushing away unexpected tears, realized that Sunday school at First Church is for all people.
- Nancy Hughen-Adams, fluent in sign language , signs for people with hearing disabilities, and her advocacy keeps the rest of us from being insensitive to the needs of the hearing-impaired .

There is no doubt that every barrier, whether physical or psychological, will be coming down at First Church. That day cannot come too soon.

Music and the Arts

Please listen to the ever-prescient Leonard Sweet:

There is also the need for postmodern Christians to be bimusical—to be able to express one's beliefs in more than one musical tradition, and to know a second musical language and tradition almost as well as one's own. . . . Postmodern communities of faith need pianos (and pianists), organs (and organists), and synthesizers (and synthesists, experts in electroacoustic music). Postmodern celebrations also need worship spaces where there is great sound, and where song leaders can open up and reach the whole person to receive the gospel in song and sermon. Song leaders should be brought back to worship and valued for their key role in building community. These song leaders are not just metronomes with a human face standing in front of towering million-dollar pipe organs. Song leaders in new paradigm faith communities see their role in celebration as body builders—breaking down barriers between people, and building bridges among the diversity of people present so that there can be two-way traffic between heaven and earth. Combining ministers of music and fine arts would also highlight the importance of aesthetics in the life of faith.[3]

Sweet is speaking of the church in the next century, but much of the future he describes has already arrived at First Church. Several items worth noting are:

Item: Worship experiences at First Church fall into two categories: formal and informal. Two worship services are formal; two are informal. We shy away from the designations "traditional" and "contemporary." Every worship service is "bimusical," incorporating both traditional and contemporary elements into the worship experience. Formal worship services are those where a carefully structured order of worship is followed, the atmosphere dignified, and the clothing of a dress-up quality. Informal worship encourages casual dress, free-flowing elements of worship, and more congregation interaction.

Item: As good Presbyterian Christians, we hold to a belief in the theological Trinity, but in addition at First Church, we celebrate an artistic trinity. The creative force behind our Music and the Arts Ministry is generated by three people: David Patrick, conductor and producer; Bryan Harden, singer and composer; George Atwell, instrumentalist and arranger. The three, well-schooled in the classics, also have spent years in the contemporary music scene. They are "bimusical" in the ultimate sense of the word. Their individual gifts, when mixed by the directing Spirit of God, provide us with significant resources in both contemporary and traditional music, plus the capability of writing, arranging, and producing our own music: anthems, hymns, and spiritual songs.

Item: Resourced by that artistic trinity, many volunteers provide us with the full array of Christian artistic expression: orchestra (ranging in age from junior high school students to musicians in their 80s); drama (including wholesome Broadway plays, youth musicals, and drama instruction for children); creative writing (including poetry, short stories, and feature articles for the newsletter and educational religious pieces); and fine arts (including exhibits featuring painters and photographers from the congregation).

Item: "What goes around comes around" so the saying goes. Years ago the church was the patron and producer of the arts. In time, secular society moved in to assume that role. Now in a time of budget cuts and reordered priorities, the production of high quality artistic expression is devolving back upon the church. Schools, which once provided solid instruction for children in music and the arts, no longer do so. The church is stepping into that breach. Rock music, often antithetical to the faith, pervades the minds of our young. It is incumbent upon the church in our time to take the rock idiom and infuse it with the gospel message. Were you to witness one of our youth concerts where the great old sanctuary of First Church is filled with flashing strobes, pounding chords, and hundreds of handclapping young people singing gospel words to a rock beat, you would understand what I mean.

We are determined to be a congregation exalting traditional music and worship while at the same time exploring new venues for the gospel in the contemporary world. The beat goes on.

John David Edington Fitness Center

When we need it most, God's guidance is especially clear. Case in point: Immediately after John David's death—in fact that very day—Trisha and I realized that we needed to designate a specific cause for memorial gifts. We wanted something that would honor our son and enhance the work of God's Son, but we did not have the time or the energy to carefully research and weigh the options. Suddenly, Trisha, under what I am now convinced was the leading of God's Spirit, suggested the creation of a fitness center in the proposed Clayton Life Center. It turned out to be an inspired choice—not our inspiration but God's. While we had no idea what would occur, God did! People from this church and from all over the country began sending gifts. Within a couple of weeks after John David's death, it became clear that the dream for a fitness center would come true. Paul writes in 1 Corinthians 6:19-20:

Or do you not know that your body is a temple of the Holy Spirit within you, which you have from God, and that you are not your own? For you were bought with a price; therefore glorify God in your body.

We took the words off the page and set them to life. Kerry Jones, our recreation minister, secured the equipment necessary and then conceived a ministry for the fitness center. It is a ministry that is now touching literally hundreds of people every week, and it is operated by volunteers. Volunteers staff the check-in desk; volunteers conduct the required orientation sessions; and volunteers provide guidance for the physical training.

From 6:00 A.M. to 10:00 P.M. every day, people of all ages are ministering to the bodies God gave them. It is thrilling, indeed, to see older people exercising to stay limber and preserve their health; to see overweight people working toward better conditioning; to see people with back trouble (I'm one of them), or bursitis, or knee problems, rehabilitating from those injuries; and to see healthy people just trying to stay that way—and all doing it as an expression of devotion to God and supplementing it with Bible studies and prayer times. In an unusual twist of God's grace, John David's death, for all the pain it is causing us, has made possible a marvelous new dimension of ministry for all ages in the John David Edington Fitness Center. Grace is sufficient.

It occurs to me that if you look back through the sampling I have just offered you, you will find two truths appear like recurring themes in a symphony: (1) the use of volunteers as initiators and leaders of programs, and, (2) the role of staff as resource persons energizing the volunteers.

Our Utilization of Facilities

Ben McKenney walked away from a good position in the business world to make the business of our church his own personal ministry. Not only has he created a business and financial operation that many other churches would love to emulate, but also he has taught us to look at the practical side of ministry from a new perspective. If I share with you his insights, perhaps your perspective will be altered as was mine.

Insight #1: Buildings are assets not liabilities. Church boards often refer to buildings as objects that divert us from the true mission of the church and that drain enormous amounts of money. At First Church we see buildings as assets used to support ministry. Make no mistake, our buildings are not shrines. We are building on Church Street in downtown Orlando, not a monument, but a mission station. Buildings are designed to be both aesthetically pleasing (they are after all built to the glory of God) and completely functional.

Insight #2: Facilities must be user-friendly. Superb programming may appeal to people, but if our facilities are not accommodating, people will stop coming. Think about it. Most buildings we enter, such as banks, fast food restaurants, offices, malls, and supermarkets are carefully designed to encourage our being there. The church should be no different. We have to meet or beat the competition.

Insight #3: The best security system is created by people and light. Downtown churches fight a never-ending battle against security problems and, as a result, many of them wind up looking like armed fortresses. We have learned that significant numbers of people coming in and going out of our church campus during all hours of the day and night (remember "the twenty-four-hour church"), combined with keeping the campus bathed in light, drives away evil deeds and people bent on doing harm.

Insight #4: *Frugal* is not a dirty word. Church finance committees are often negatively characterized as "bean counters." Not fair. What a gift it is to have people who keep one eye focused on the nickel-and-dime ways we waste our money, and the other eye focused on creative ways we can spend money to enhance our ministry. Ostentation in the church is anathema to God. At First Church we keep buildings beautiful and we do programs well, but we do not overdo either one. Our unwritten guide is this: When in doubt, spend it on people.

Who says "You can't be all things to all people"? First Presbyterian Church, by God's grace and with God's help, is being all things to all people, 24-7-365!

CHAPTER VII

INVITATION:
Expediting Inviting Is Exciting

When it comes to Jesus' great banquet, Rita Pierson is "the hostess with the mostest." You know about Jesus' great banquet. It is drawn from the parable he told in Luke 14:16-23 (RSV):

But he said to him, "A man once gave a great banquet, and invited many; and at the time for the banquet he sent his servant to say to those who had been invited, 'Come; for all is now ready.' But they all alike began to make excuses. The first said to him, 'I have bought a field, and I must go out and see it; I pray you, have me excused.' And another said, 'I have bought five yoke of oxen, and I go to examine them; I pray you, have me excused.' And another said, 'I have married a wife, and therefore I cannot come.' So the servant came and reported this to his master. Then the householder in anger said to his servant, 'Go out quickly to the streets and lanes of the city, and bring in the poor and maimed and blind and lame.' And the servant said, 'Sir, what you commanded has been done, and still there is room.' And the master said to the servant, 'Go out to the highways and hedges, and compel people to come in, that my house may be filled.'"

At First Church we take the command of Christ to, "Go out to the highways and hedges and compel people to come in, so that my house may be filled" with utmost seriousness."

While you may know the parable of the great banquet, you might not know Rita Pierson. She is our version of Pearl Mesta. Back in the 1950s before scandals and assassinations put a hard edge on Washington politics, "political parties" had a double meaning. There were the Democratic and

Republican parties all right, but there were also the social bashes that dotted the evening hours. Some said more political good was done at those parties than in the halls of Congress. Pearl Mesta earned a reputation for herself by throwing the best and most popular parties. She was called the "hostess with the mostest," and an invitation to one of her parties was a cherished item, and one not to be declined. When it comes to evangelism, Rita Pierson, is our "hostess with the mostest."

Rita Pierson, whose early years in the Roman Catholic Church prepared her to be a superb Presbyterian, has been a prime force in our evangelism ministry. By using the resources of Ben Johnson, Columbia Seminary's Professor of Evangelism, she developed our Friendmakers program, which is enabling us to make swift, nonthreatening, and winsome contact with visitors to our congregation. She and all of our Friendmakers corps resonate with Jesus' description of the Kingdom as a joyous feast and party. Their spirit has infected the rest of us at First Church. Since the Christian life is the happiest experience we can offer another human being, extending invitations to the Kingdom is our top priority.

Theologian Robert Hotchkins of the University of Chicago writes:

Christians ought to be celebrating constantly. We ought to be preoccupied with parties, banquets, feasts, and merriment. We ought to give ourselves over to celebrations of joy because we have been liberated from the fear of life and the fear of death. We ought to attract people to the church quite literally by the sheer pleasure there is in being a Christian. [1]

Rita Pierson invites other people to share the joy of the Kingdom experience better than anyone else I know. Under the influence of her inviting spirit, we at First Church attempt to frame everything we do under the invitation to the feast. I share Rita Pierson's passion for evangelism. I believe that lost people matter to God. That is not just a clever cliché; it is the driving passion of my life, and it has been the driving passion of my life for more than a quarter of a century. I believe there is a real heaven, a place of eternal union with God; and I believe there is a real hell, a place of eternal separation from God. I believe we are going to one place or the other. So if there is an air of urgency and intensity to my preaching, it is because I am struggling to be a channel by which the Spirit of God can reach the nonbeliever and the casual believer. And if there is a determination on the part of our church to extend the invitation to Kingdom-living to as many people as possible, it is because we long to share with them the joy of knowing that they are heaven-bound.

I identify with John Welsh, a great Scottish preacher of another day, who at night would kneel by his bed and pray for his people. His wife would say, "Come to bed, John, it's too cold." He would reply, "Dear, I have the souls of 3,000 to answer for and I do not know how it is with many of them." I echo his words. I have nearly 5,000 souls to answer for and I do not know how it is with many of them.

Some suggest that I am a bit of a fanatic about all of this. I came across one wag's definition of a fanatic: "A fanatic is a person who can't change his mind and won't change the subject." When it comes to people and their relationship with Christ, I cannot change my mind and I will not change the subject. I shall preach Jesus Christ, calling people to surrender their lives to him and inviting them to claim their eternal destiny. Happily for me, and for our great old downtown church, many of our people feel the same way.

Guiding Principles

You do not have to scratch too deeply below the surface of our church to find the guiding principles for our invitational evangelism ministry.

Principle #1 - You can't share what you don't know.
We are living in a time that is calling us to proclaim the claims of Christ more powerfully than ever before. Loren Mead writes:

No longer can we assume that everyone is a Christian. No longer does the community, through schools, festivals, associations, and standards reinforce Christian values and beliefs. No longer are we living in a society which encourages the growth and development and the spread of the church. In the years ahead people will not be Christians because they were born in Christian homes, or because their parents were Christian, or because being a Christian is the socially acceptable thing to do. Instead, to be a Christian is going to require a conscious and costly choice, a deliberate and difficult decision.[2]

Pointed words. However, before we can invite someone else to make that choice, we have to have a deep, fresh, vibrant experience of Jesus Christ in our own lives. Be careful now. I am not referring here to some kind of emotional spasm that may mean something today or next week but will be forgotten next month or next year. No, I'm talking about something infinitely deeper and infinitely more dynamic. I am talking about saying quietly, genuinely, sincerely, "Lord Jesus, I offer myself to you, nothing held back." That is not an act of emotion; it is an act of will. If we are shy in talking about Jesus with others, then chances are it is because we are shy of a vibrant experience of Jesus in our own lives. You can't share what you don't know.

Principle #2 - You can't win people you don't love.
Look it up for yourself in 1 John 3:14. "We know that we have passed from death to life because we love one another." To believe in Jesus is to desire to share his gospel, and to believe in Jesus is to love other people. Put them together, and this is what you get: You can't win people you don't love. I want to say something now that might seem a bit shocking, but not to other Presbyterians. I do not believe that God calls

us to seek to win every single person we meet along our life's way. Instead, I believe God calls us to win those people whom he has prepared for us. To borrow the image of Jesus, we need to scatter the seed of the gospel indiscriminately. That means that a generic invitation must be delivered to every home and to every heart, even if that invitation is simply addressed "Occupant." That is the primary function of the church—to deliver an all-encompassing invitation. But when it comes to our individual efforts, the focus ought to be narrow to heighten its effectiveness. Jesus said, "See how the fields are ripe for harvesting." But for many of us, our "fields" might extend no farther than the circle of our acquaintances. Within the contacts we have with people each day in the normal course of our living, there are plenty of people who need to hear, who need to receive, the invitation to Christlike living. We do not have to go to those people and beat them over the head with our Bible. Instead, we begin to pray for those people every day. We spend time with them. We develop a good relationship with them. We demonstrate to them that we love them and care for them. By so doing, we earn the right to be heard. You can't win people you don't love.

Principle #3 - You can't give what you don't have.

What people need more than anything else today is to know that they matter to the Almighty. They need to know that they are loved by God so much that he gave his only Son for them. They need to know that they matter to you and are loved by you. In other words, they need mercy. But you can't give what you don't have. Therefore, as we invite others to become a part of the family of the Lord, we need not be harsh and judgmental. We need not be coercive or overbearing or overly pious. We need not be dominating or intimidating or manipulating. All we need to be is kind and merciful. Lloyd Ogilvie once reminded me that in Genesis, when Jacob was helping his sons load provisions for the trip to Egypt, Jacob said to them, "Put in a little honey." Type that into your mental teleprompter. When you are sharing the good news of God's Son with others, when you are inviting others to Kingdom-living, always put in a little honey! People are won by gracious, warm, loving acceptance. God must have believed that, too, for God came into this world as the kindest, most loving, most grace-filled person who ever lived. If we approach others with merciful kindness, gracious warmth, and accepting love, they will respond by knocking on the doors of our hearts, demanding to know the reason for the faith that is in us, and demanding to know the Savior who has so transformed us. You can't give what you don't have.

Practical Applications

At First Church the invitation to faith involves several practical and successive steps.

1. Worship. At the conclusion of every worship service, without fail, we extend what we call the *invitation to Christian discipleship.* We keep it short, simple, clear, and to the point. Usually it sounds like this:

If you have never made your personal commitment in faith to Jesus Christ as the Savior and Lord of your life, then I invite you to consider making that commitment of faith today. You do not have to understand all there is to know about Jesus. That can come later. The first step is to say, "Lord Jesus, I want to be yours." Take that step today and your life will be changed. If, at some point previously in your life, you have made that faith commitment to Christ and today you wish to unite with this church and become a part of this family of the faith, then I urge you to take that step of commitment as well. In either case, once this worship service concludes, make your way forward to the chancel steps. One of the ministers will be here to receive you. In the name of Jesus, I bid you, "Come."

Our elders meet after every single worship service to formally receive those who have responded to the invitation. There follows a time for the sharing of one's spiritual journey, and for professing or reaffirming one's faith in Jesus

Christ. This very special time is concluded with prayer and celebration. As I look back over the last ten years I can count on the fingers of one hand the very few occasions when no one responded to that invitation. Sidebar: An extra blessing in this whole process is that our elders find their own faith strengthened and renewed by hearing the stories of those whom the Lord brings to us.

2. Friendmakers. A group of fifty men and women, known as Friendmakers, constitute our frontline point of contact with those whom God brings to us. What do they do? A sample week will give you a clue: Prior to each worship service, Friendmakers serve in the narthex to greet visitors and to give them packets of church information. After each worship service, a small group of Friendmakers collect the signed slips from the *Ritual of Friendship* booklets. These people, lovingly called "Holy Tearers," tear the slips from the booklets and separate the slips into categories of "visitors" and "members." On Sunday afternoon, from noon until 3:00, the names of new visitors and the attendance of returning visitors are entered into the computer.

The work started on Sunday is completed over the next three days by various volunteers. All first-time visitors receive a letter from me and an invitation to return. Out-of-town visitors also receive a letter from me expressing gratitude for sharing our worship experience. Repeat visitors trigger a process that includes telephone calls from Friendmakers and staff members, the church newsletter, invitations to Visitors' Dinners, and personal visits when requested. We tend to place primary emphasis on telephone and mail contact because our church draws people from all over central Florida, many of them living significant distances from the church. Furthermore, given the circumstances of the society in which we live, personal visits are appropriate and beneficial only when requested. To quote Rita Pierson, "The Friendmakers' sole purpose is to be a friend in Christ to those new friends whom Christ brings to our church."

3. Visitors' Dinners. Every six weeks we invite those who have visited the church to come to dinner in our Lee Fellowship Hall. My wife, Trisha, and I serve as hosts, but we also have both Friendmakers and staff members present. We average sixty to eighty visitors per dinner—add in the staff members and the Friendmakers and the dinner totals approximately 120. I am convinced, however, that regardless of the numbers involved, the strategy of the dinner will work. Dinner is preceded by a time of visiting informally. Trisha and I make a point to meet every visitor personally.

A seated dinner follows. The food is always delicious; the fellowship even better. Each table of eight has a mixture of visitors, Friendmakers, and staff, and the mealtime is spent chatting about the church and its activities. The program after the meal includes a ten-minute video presentation featuring interviews with church members and glimpses of our ministries. Because we have over 150 different ministries under the umbrella of First Church, the video provides a quick overview, giving visitors what we hope is a tantalizing look at our church's life. I then deliver a "State of Our Church" address concluding with the invitation to commitment to Christ and to membership in our church. Once again, as always when the invitation is given, some of our elders are present and are ready to formally receive those who respond to the invitation. We have never had a visitors' dinner without having people profess their faith or join the church afterwards. The church underwrites the dinner, but the new members derived from the dinner more than offset the cost. Try it; you'll like it!

4. Seekers and Joiners. Under that title we conduct a six-week class that recycles throughout the year. Attendance is optional, but is strongly encouraged for visitors who are interested in learning more about our church and for people who have recently joined our congregation. Under the general leadership of Kent Sterchi, who has a heart for evangelism and a love for people, each class focuses on a different theme and features time with a different staff member. Here is the class schedule:

Week 1: Worship. The class focuses on the centrality of worship in the believer's experience, including both corporate and individual worship.

Week 2: Study. The emphasis is placed on the study of the Scripture and the educational opportunities available in our church.

Week 3: Serve. Class members are called to serve Christ in our church and in our world and are shown ways of accomplishing that goal.

Week 4: Share. A practical experience in learning how to share the faith in word and in deed, together with investing time, talent, and treasure in the work of the church.

Week 5: Time with the senior minister. I share with the class my vision for the church's future and then respond to any questions that they desire to address to me. This is great fun for me.

Week 6: Celebration. The class joins together with members of our Session for a service of Holy Communion. During the service those in the class who wish to do so are formally received into the membership of the church.

Postscript: People who attend Seekers and Joiners move through the six-week cycle in a small group that includes at least a couple of people who are already church members. We have discovered that this experience helps new people develop an instant bond with the church.

Enduring Results

Jesus spoke of "the harvest," and we speak of "results," but we mean the same thing. The delivery of the invitation is our responsibility; the response to the invitation is God's. God brings the harvest; God brings the results. We simply invite and then God, by the power of the Holy Spirit working in human lives, draws people to make their life-changing, death-defeating commitment to Christ and the church. But while we do not bring the results, we do count them. Numbers matter. As Peter Drucker once said in a conference, "We count people because people count." Every number represents a priceless human soul. Please, therefore, do not tell me that numbers are not important.

What does amaze me is the rich variety of people who respond to the invitation and become enfolded into our particular body of Christ.

We are seeing different kinds of people. Presbyterians usually draw only a small slice of the demographic pie, but I can tell you that slice is widened in our downtown church. The invitation delivered to all is having the effect of adding to our number people from a variety of ethnic and cultural backgrounds. To stand in our pulpit now on any given Sunday and look out on our congregation is to behold a rich diversity of God's people.

For example, last Sunday about ten pews back I saw the chairman of the board of a local bank sitting next to "Dr. John." Dr. John—now there is a story. Emily Dickinson has a line that reads "tell all the truth, but tell it slant." With a minor alteration, I could apply that line to Dr. John: "live all of life, but live it slant." He comes at life from a different perspective than most of us. Apparently at one time he was a professor with a Ph.D. degree. A series of mental and emotional struggles left him unable to cope with the demands of a normal life. He took to the streets, ultimately ending up on our streets. He lives as a vagabond in this tropical paradise. I shall never forget the first time he came to see me. He had attended church, been warmly welcomed and had heard the invitation. Now he wanted to talk about belonging to Christ and belonging to our church. He walked into my office carrying all his earthly goods on his back and it was obvious he was some extended time removed from a good bath. One side of his face was clean shaven; the other side of his face sported a full beard. I said to him, "Dr. John, we're going to talk about Christ in a moment, but first you have to answer one question for me. Why in the world do you have a beard on one side of your face and the other side is shaved?"

He said, "It's like that because that's who I am . . . half straight and half wild." Now do you see why I say he lives life at a slant?

What I discovered, and what the people who sit on our pews have discovered, is that the circle of friends in Jesus Christ can be drawn wide enough to include everyone and anyone! I am absolutely persuaded that one of the secrets of the dynamism of First Church is the incredible array of people embraced within its walls.

We are receiving people from many denominations. The day of denominational loyalty is done. People no longer join a church because of a denominational name out front. They join a church because of the spirit and the people they find inside. In fact, as I look at the denominations in our country today, most of them are in various stages of decay or disintegration. I suspect that in another fifteen to twenty years denominations, as we know them, will no longer exist. Leonard Sweet, whose crystal ball seems clearer than most, suggests that, in the future, denominations will fade and churches will operate in "netweaves" woven together by a common understanding and expression of worship and mission, minus the baggage of bureaucracies and hierarchies. What is happening nationally is happening even more rapidly locally, and I see it on our church pews. Virtually every denomination in America today has a representative on the membership rolls of First Church. Even our ministerial staff, which now includes a Baptist and an Episcopalian, reflects that reality. Frankly, I think the Lord is proud of that. "We are one in the Spirit; we are one in the Lord."

We are receiving people of different ages. John Rife, whose buoyant faith inspires my own, is fond of saying to me:

When you came here in 1982, I could stand in the back of our sanctuary on Sunday and it looked like a sea of silver. Now I stand in the back on Sunday morning and the sanctuary looks like a can of worms—children and young people everywhere, the place throbbing with movement and excitement.

His observation is correct. To paraphrase what has become a classic line from the movie *Field of Dreams*, "If you preach it, they will come." In Jesus-language: "If I am lifted up, I will draw all people to me." Whatever else we do right or wrong, the thing we do best in this old downtown church is to proclaim the exciting, inviting gospel of Jesus Christ. Like a magnet dropped onto a pile of iron filings, the message draws people of all ages, even, and especially, those who are young.

When placing this entire dimension of our ministry under a microscope, we might focus upon one instant that captures the whole. One Sunday, after our early worship service, five people had responded to the invitation. I joined our elders in the Heritage Center, adjacent to the sanctuary, to receive these people into our church. As the five of them shared their stories, I found myself gripped with increasing awe.

There was a young couple—mid-thirties, well dressed, obviously building lives marked by earthly success. The husband was holding in his arms a precious little girl. They told a story of growing up with no church background and no real understanding of the faith. They were driven primarily by the pursuits of position and possessions. Now God had given them the gift of this child. Suddenly they realized that they wanted the child to grow up in a healthier, more spiritual atmosphere. They decided that they wanted to find a church. Having learned of our church through television, they had visited on several occasions. They had learned enough about Christ here to make the decision to offer themselves to him.

There was another young couple—late twenties, more casually dressed, also holding a child, a bright eyed little boy, in their arms. They began to share with us the fact that they had grown up in Christian homes, and had been Christians and church members since childhood. They had moved to Orlando seeking work, had found positions, and now were struggling to make ends meet. They, too, wanted a church home for themselves, but especially for their child.

The fifth person was a young man, twenty-two years of age, looking and feeling a trifle uncomfortable. Here is the story he told:

I grew up in a home with an alcoholic, abusive father. Discipline in my home consisted of a full martial arts exercise, and I was always on the receiving end. At seventeen I ran away from home. Since then I have lived on the streets of New York City, Dallas, and New Orleans. I have slept on more dirty sidewalks and eaten more meals from dumpsters than I can count. Somewhere along the way someone stuck a Bible in my hand. I've spent the last couple of months trying to read it. I hitched rides down here to Florida, thinking the weather might be better for sleeping on the street. This last week, to avoid the rains that I hadn't counted on, I went to the Rescue Mission. They've helped me a lot: I have a cot to sleep on, three hot meals a day, and a job in their thrift store. They've also helped me learn about Jesus. They suggested that I come to this church today, because at this church I would be welcomed and accepted. That is true. So I want to straighten my life out and get right with the Lord.

By the way, one of our elders present that Sunday was Dwight Sample. Because of his job as a retail manager, he has to work many Sundays and is rarely able to attend these sessions. However, he was there this particular Sunday— you would not dare say that God was not responsible for that, would you?—and he leaned over to me and whispered, "I'll see to it that the young man gets the clothes he needs."

I looked at the five new members, compared their stories and thought to myself, "Only the Spirit of God could make this happen." Put all of that on the slide under your microscope, examine it carefully, and you will see the downtown church at full power.

Our inviting-Christ calls us to be inviting-people. Our people, as they consciously and deliberately invite friends to try our church, have been an exciting aspect of our growth. Even my son, John David, helped to foster that inviting atmosphere. Trisha and I, in the midst of all that was going on just hours after we learned of John David's death, had a card placed in our hands. It was written by Susan Bales. She and her husband, Clint, have been good friends and devoted church members. The card read:

Dear Howard and Trisha,

Clint and I want to extend our deepest sympathy on the loss of your son this morning. On December 11, Sunday before last, as a Friendmaker, I was interviewing one of the new members of our church, Heather Gray. I asked her how she managed to find her way to First Presbyterian Church. She told me that when she was searching for a church, John David told her, "Why don't you go to my Dad's church." I never got to see John David and thank him for sending us this wonderful new member. But I just wanted you to know how he touched her life and so many others as a witness for our church. May God bless and strengthen you.

Love,

Susan

John David's inviting spirit, multiplied by hundreds and hundreds of others at First Church, has given this church the energy it needs to pursue new vision, new hope, and new direction. I have so many things to thank John David for.

Add one more.

CHAPTER VIII

INSPIRATION:
How Shall They Hear?

William Faulkner, the bard of the South, once said of sin, "You ain't got to: you just can't help it."

In a daring leap of logic, I want to apply Faulkner's homey wisdom on the subject of sin to the subject of preaching in the downtown church: "You ain't got to; you just can't help it." In other words, the downtown church will not fall without strong preaching, but it cannot rise without it either. Over the past ten years, our evangelism team has kept a running tabulation of the factors that draw people into the life of our congregation. Consistently in the tabulation, second and third places have rotated among the different aspects of the church's ministry such as the youth ministry, the children's ministry, the television ministry, the Basics Sunday School Class, and the weekday kindergarten. First place, however, has remained unchanged: the preaching of God's Word. So preaching is not all of it, but it is, oh, so important.

Let me clearly assert that in a downtown church preaching cannot be conducted in a vacuum. It must draw its energy from the church's people and programs while at the same time it provides the inspiration to energize the church's ministry to the world around it. Drawn as a picture, if the various ministries of the downtown church are the spokes of a wheel, preaching is its hub. Perhaps the best way for me to make that case is to share with you something of how I preach and something of how I prepare to preach.

I preach authoritatively. My own authority? Good heavens, no. The authority of the Scriptures themselves? Absolutely. The late Bruce Thielemann, distinguished preaching minister at the First Presbyterian Church of Pittsburgh, Pennsylvania, once defined preaching as, "God's redeeming act in Jesus Christ lived again for personal, present encounter." His definition of preaching informs my own.

The obvious reality of preaching—a person preparing a sermon and stepping into a pulpit and delivering it—does not begin to capture the true dynamic of it all. There is a spiritual dimension of preaching far surpassing that simple human reality. Preaching is not the delivery of an essay on the preacher's philosophy of life, though inevitably one's life-view will bleed through the lines of the sermon. Preaching is not a theological lecture, though all good preaching has sound and significant theology within it. Preaching is not the teaching of Christian morality, though all good preaching will encourage adherence to the moral standards of our Christ. Preaching is not the stringing together of Bible verses or stories, though all good preaching will be firmly, solidly rooted and grounded in the Scripture. Preaching is all of those things; and yet it is more than all of those things, and it is more than any of those things. It is nothing less than God's redeeming act in Jesus Christ lived again for personal, present encounter.

What God did for humankind through Christ on Calvary, by some mysterious power of the Holy Spirit, God repeats when the story is told by one seeking to be a clear and open channel for that Spirit. As a result, those listening to the sermon might as well be standing at the foot of the cross, because they shall have to confront all over again for the very first time the saving sacrifice of Jesus Christ. Therefore, when the preacher stands to speak, the words are delivered under no less an authority than the authority of God Almighty.

My professor of preaching in seminary carved that truth into my consciousness in such a way that I have never been able to forget it. Whenever one of us would-be preachers in his class would be assigned to deliver a sermon as a class exercise, he would stand in the back of the room, leaning against the wall, arms folded, ice-blue eyes frozen on the one preaching. When we would come to the end of the sermon, almost without exception, he would suddenly explode from the back of the room with the deafening cry, "Where is your gospel? Where is your gospel?" While the experience would shatter our composure and intimidate our spirit, that was simply the short-term result. The long-term result was that not one of us who sat at his feet has ever forgotten that when we stand on our feet to preach, we must deliver in some way and in some word the true message of the gospel. Preaching is God's redeeming act in Jesus Christ lived again for personal, present encounter. Therefore, when I preach, I preach authoritatively.

I preach compulsively. The preacher must always be under the compulsion of a call. You do not ever drift into the pulpit. If you do, you do not stay very long. Preaching is not a job you want. Preaching is not a job you seek. The more I study the lives of the greatest preachers the more I realize that they felt a sense of personal unworthiness for the calling that was theirs. Moses did not want the job; Amos did not want the job; Jeremiah did not want the job. Preaching is not a job you want. It is not a job you seek. It is a job to which you are called. There must be gnawing away at your insides, a feeling that says, "Woe unto me if I do not preach the gospel."

I have been preaching for more than twenty-five years, and I tell you that I am terrified to stand in front of people to speak. I am, at my core, a shy and reserved person. Therefore, on Sundays I cannot step through the door, into the chancel, and up to the pulpit on my own. This may or may not sound a little strange, but I feel—literally feel—a shove in the small of my back. My guess is that if you were standing behind me at that moment you would see my pulpit robe move. Something—better word, *Someone*—stronger than I am takes hold of me and literally pushes me into the pulpit. I cannot do it alone. Preaching is not a job you seek. It is a job to which you are called. You must have the deep inner conviction that you are doing precisely what God wants you to do. The Word of God in your heart must burn like a fire in your bones. The prophet Jeremiah knew the compulsion. To be a preacher is to live under the compulsion of God's call.

I preach passionately. Preaching is strenuous. It demands everything you have: everything in your mind; everything in your heart; everything in your body. It must be passionate. The people must know that it comes straight out of your own struggle in the faith. Of course, when you are dealing with the most exciting, the most engaging, the most energizing message the world has ever heard, how could you ever treat it as "just another day at the office"? When my son, John David, was in kindergarten, his teacher asked him, "What does your daddy do?" John David, with that childlike innocence Jesus always celebrated, replied, "He stands up in church and screams and shouts!" In my case, there is probably more than a measure of truth to what he said. However, let me quickly declare that while screaming and shouting are not so important, passion is. The passion must show. When you analyze the methods of communication employed by the only true master preacher, Jesus, you find passion—strong, unequivocal, unreserved passion—flowing in, through, over, under, and around every word.

Preaching, quite literally, consumes you. Your weekends become the time when your stomach is filled with butterflies and your nerves are set on a ragged edge. You are up on Sundays, perhaps before the sun, to study, honing your mind razor sharp, and to pray, fixing your heart on the Son. Then in the uplifting context of worship, you proceed to pour everything you have and everything you are into the act of preaching so, when it is over, you feel you have been used and used up. You are spent. There is nothing left. My beloved professor, James Stewart of Scotland, used to say, "Every sermon well preached will cause you to die a little." True.

Truer than true. Truly preach the Word of God and you will shorten your life a little bit.

This is not to suggest that the preacher is all of it or that the preacher is any of it. The preacher is not. Preaching is God's redeeming act lived again, but I submit that God acts through preaching that is built upon the Word of God and to which the preacher is utterly given, utterly surrendered. It must be passionate.

I preach personally. Robert Kirkpatrick in *The Creative Delivery of Sermons* wrote, "The power of a sermon is measured at the point of contact with the pew."[1] Therefore, my preaching, designed to make that point of contact, is personal in nature—personal for the listener and personal for the preacher.

My preaching is personal for the listener. My preaching flows out of my pastoral care. I work tirelessly to stay in touch with people, keeping my finger upon the pulse of their hopes and dreams, their fears and frustrations, their sins and shortcomings, their sufferings and sorrows. Since there is nothing more foolish than the answer to an unasked question, and since there is nothing more absurd than the solution to a nonexistent problem, I tremble to step into any pulpit without having taken some measure of the life experience of those to whom I shall be preaching.

The practice of preaching in our time is undergoing seismic changes. Leonard Sweet measures those changes on his own personal "Richter Scale" shared in his book *FaithQuakes*. Catch the vibration from his words:

Homiletics specialists are inclined to recommend shorter and shorter sermons to accommodate postmoderns' shorter and shorter attention spans. Charles L. Rice, whose text on preaching wants us to "make less" of preaching so that the world can "make more" of it, argues that since the longest television viewers go without a break is fourteen minutes, sermons should stay within the fifteen-minute range.

But the question is not so much how long the sermon goes as

how goes the sermon. People who sit down to hear a sermon do so with different expectations than when they sit down to watch a soap opera. In African American traditions of preaching, which are highly interactive, participatory, metaphorical, and performative, sermons can go on for hours without diminishment of attention because something is "happening." Fifteen-minute sermons that are linear, point-making, position-taking and intellectualist are fourteen minutes too long. [2]

In order to ensure that something "happens" when the Word of God is preached at First Church, I ask—I consistently ask— people to share with me their suggestions for preaching topics. Furthermore, when I anticipate addressing a specific subject that I know is reflective of the experience of some of them, I ask them in advance to send me their specific insights into that subject. Those letters not only become fodder for my own preparation, but they also guarantee the powerful contact point between pulpit and pew.

As an aside, I am aware in my preaching that a large portion of our congregation each week is made up of children. Aubrey Brown, writing in *Presbyterian Outlook* asks:

How many times have you cringed when profound spiritual or biblical concepts have been presented to children in stark physical or allegorical terms? Good educators have dealt helpfully with concerns like this for generations. And vocabularies! Not many ministers can talk easily in words that children can understand. [3]

Because what he says is so on target, each of my sermons uses the simplest language possible, employs clear signposts making it possible for children to follow the logic of the message, and includes, without fail, at least one story or point or illustration that any young child can fully understand and appreciate. At First Church, through our Children's Ministry, we work very hard not only to encourage our children to attend worship, but also to educate them for participation in worship. My preaching is personal and personalized for the listener.

The other meaning I attach to the spoken word has to do with my own life's experience. Whether the pulpit is clear Plexiglas or solid wood, the one standing in the pulpit must be transparent. The people who sit in the pews must be able to identify with the preacher. If I am unwilling to crack open the door of my heart and my life and grant them entrance, then we shall never experience true communion and communication. To be sure, abusing that personal privilege by parading ad nauseam the details of one's personal life is a grievous sin both against God and against the people of God. However, sensitive, discreet, restrained, and appropriate personal revelations that point to the ultimate revelation of God in Christ can magnetize one's proclamation. In fact, John Claypool, who has skillfully calculated a proper balance for personal stories in preaching, has this to say:

We will make our greatest impact in preaching when we dare to make available to the woundedness of others what we have learned through grappling with our own woundedness.[4]

In ways that I do not fully understand, but that seem to me to be abundantly clear in the unfolding pages of this book, the death of our son John David, a singular event of terrible sorrow, has had an unintended, unexpected by-product: the highlighting of so many unique dimensions of life in the downtown church. My preaching ministry at First Church is one more example. The sermon I preached after his death, as purely personal a sermon as I have ever preached, turned out to be one where the contact point between pulpit and pew nearly overpowered us all. That sermon is included in this book, not only as an illustration of the kind of "personal preaching" to which I refer, but also because it became one more galvanizing element in binding my story and this church's story together.

In preaching, the personal life of the preacher must show through like the glow of a lamp shows through shuttered windows. A preacher's life, if touched by the Spirit of God, can touch listeners' hearts and lives with God's light. For example, Dr. Kyung Chik Han is one of the best loved and most respected Christians in all of Korea. He is the founding pastor of the Young Nak Presbyterian Church in Seoul, now the largest Presbyterian Church in the world. He was a pastor in North Korea when the communists took over. He paid an unbelievably heavy price for his faith. At last, he managed a miraculous escape to South Korea and established that great church in Seoul. He is held in awe and reverence in Korea. When I preached in that church several years ago, Dr. Han invited Trisha and me to be his guests for Sunday dinner after the five worship services. The great man, now in his eighties, lost his wife to death some years back and lives alone. He suggested that we walk to a restaurant several blocks away. The sidewalks of Seoul were, as usual, jammed with people. As we walked along, when the people saw it was Dr. Han, they would quietly step aside, drop into silence, and simply stretch out their hands to brush the edge of his coat, as if they were trying to draw some of his vast spiritual power. It was an extraordinary thing to witness, yet Dr. Han, chatting amiably with us, seemed to be totally unaware of what was happening. The people of Seoul, struck silent by the power of Dr. Han's sacrificial life, reminded me that the quality of one's preaching will be determined in significant measure by the quality of one's life. The old saw cuts right to the truth: "He preaches well who lives well."

I preach purposefully. Here, for whatever it may be worth, is a very practical word on the way I prepare to preach. This method results from both fear and frustration. When I began preaching on Sunday mornings to those marvelous (and long-suffering) saints in Kilgore, Texas, I would confront, by that afternoon, the sickening thought that all that was in me had been poured out in that morning's sermon. What in the world was I going to preach about next week? The ceaseless pressure of preaching week by week began to tyrannize my schedule and terrorize my soul. Clearly, unless something changed I would either bomb out or burn out! Some years ago, Dr. Edgar Gammon of Myers Park Presbyterian Church in Charlotte, North Carolina, stepped into his pulpit one Sunday morning and without so much as one word of warning, resigned his position. In the ensuing press coverage, a reporter asked Dr. Gammon what had led to his sudden resignation. Gammon wearily replied, "The relentless return of the Sabbath." It was that same relentless pressure that backed me into the system I use to this day.

My preaching now has plan and purpose. I work in one-year blocks of time beginning in July of each year. For the past year I have maintained a file titled "sermon ideas," into which have been placed file notes and clippings drawn from my devotional study of the Bible, my reading, my conversations with and correspondence from members of the congregation, and my exposure to the issues impacting people's lives, our city, and our world. I take two weeks in July to sift through that accumulated mass of material, searching for themes, topics, needs and issues that could profitably be addressed from the pulpit. Then under the thematic guidance of the Christian Year and the seasonal emphases unique to our church, I develop a "sermon nugget" for each Sunday of the upcoming year.

The next step is incredibly important and it has three parts:
1. Do basic work researching the biblical text for each sermon.
2. Develop a rough, working outline for the sermon itself.
3. Decide on a title—one with a hook that catches attention.

I then prepare a folder for each sermon by title. The title becomes the mental hook for me in developing that sermon. Once I have the title in my mind (that is the reason a catchy title is so essential for me), I find that while reading, even pleasure reading, items will appear that will be helpful in some future sermon. I make the necessary notes and drop them in the file.

Perhaps an example might be helpful: During this past summer's preparation cycle, I was developing a sermon entitled "No God, No Peace—Know God, Know Peace!" It was based on the story of King Saul who enjoyed a wealth of personal talent and an abundant success. Yet, unable to handle the success that came to him, he wound up throwing himself on his own sword—a hopeless, hapless, helpless suicide. In subsequent days, my normal reading yielded up two contemporary situations much like Saul's. *Sports Illustrated* carried the story of Sarah Devens, the best female athlete Dartmouth College ever had. Yet the extraordinary success that she enjoyed delivered more pressure than she could bear. At age twenty-one, about to begin her senior year, she took her own life. Just days later I picked up the *New York Times Magazine.* There unfolded the story of Robert O'Donnell who, in 1987, successfully rescued Baby Jessica McClure from a well in Midland, Texas. The first flush of attention derived from his success excited him. But gradually the success turned from a blessing into a burden, and, in 1995, Robert O'Donnell shot himself on a west Texas road. These stories were immediately clipped and placed in the file to be used later in the actual writing of the sermon.

As the year unfolds, I work on three sermons at a time. On Tuesday of each week, I pull out the file for the sermon scheduled three weeks hence, review the material, rework the outline, plumb for weak spots, and schedule further research where it will be needed. Each Wednesday I pull the file for the sermon to be preached in two weeks and write a rough draft— unpolished, almost always too long, somewhat disorganized. Thursday and Friday I take the rough draft for the upcoming sermon, edit it, polish it, and write out the text in full. Having written to that extent, I have embedded in my mind the outline and flow of the sermon.

Portions of Saturday and early Sunday morning are then spent internalizing, not memorizing, the sermon. It is not a rote exercise; it is a dynamic process. By "internalization" I mean that I become a part of the material prepared, and it becomes a part of me. Therefore, when I stand in the pulpit, under the power of the Spirit, it is a matter of opening both my brain and my heart and letting the sermon flow.

The benefits of this system have proved enormous for me. As I hoped and expected, it released me from the pressure of "the relentless return of the Sabbath." Another benefit, unexpected but most welcome, has been the ability of a preaching plan to draw the various dimensions of our church's ministry into a coherent and coordinated whole.

Once again a specific example could prove enlightening. A couple of years ago my preaching plan was to include a series of sermons under the general title "Families Under Fire: Issues That Divide and Faith That Unites." The sermons would deal with subjects such as abuse, divorce, bigotry, pornography, infidelity, and abortion. Since the preaching plan was widely disseminated, all of our church resources were applied to the preaching dynamic. Our Christian Education Department developed Growth Classes and short-term Sunday school studies related to the designated topics. The music staff developed worship services and surrounded each sermon with appropriate music, even to the point of creating original hymns directly tied to each subject. I solicited letters from members of the congregation asking them to share with me both their thoughts and their experiences in these areas, receiving responses in the hundreds. Our evangelism ministry used the series as a trigger for special outreach into the community. At the conclusion of each worship service, our Church Street Counseling Center provided their Christian therapists in order to meet with individuals seeking spiritual counseling related to these services. During those weeks, fifty-two individuals sought help, healing, and hope through this ministry.

In this particular instance the preaching of the Word allowed us to marshal the various dimensions of our ministry into a coherent, coordinated effort to transform people and to overcome their problems through the power of Jesus Christ. It was, I believe, an example of the downtown church functioning at its very best. However, it could never have happened had there been no plan and purpose to the pulpit ministry.

The downtown church will not fall without strong preaching, but it cannot rise without it either. One of my mentors in the faith, Dr. John Leith, Pemberton Professor of Theology at Union Theological Seminary in Virginia, put it in his book *An Introduction to the Reformed Tradition*:

The Christian community forfeits its own greatest opportunity when it minimizes the significance of preaching. The effectiveness of preaching is difficult to measure. Yet it is a documentable fact that over a period of years the quality of preaching determines in significant measure the quality of a congregation's life. [5]

Or, as Paul asked about the Christians in Rome: "And how are they to believe in one of whom they have not heard? And how are they to hear one without someone to proclaim him?" How indeed?

I preached the following sermon when I returned to the pulpit after the death of my son, John David.

SERMON

When the Waters Are Deep: 1 Corinthians 13:13

King David once said: "There is but one step between me and death."

Just one step. Tell me about it. On a stormy night, in the first hours of December 21, my son, my only son, John David, took that one step. On streets made slick by driving rain, he lost control of his car and crashed into a tree. In an instant, the candle of a life that had burned for twenty-two years was snuffed out. There is but one step between me and death, King David said. Just one step.

The telephone ringing jolted us out of a deep sleep. The voice on the other end said, "There are Orlando policemen at your door, please let them in." Foreboding began to rise like floodwaters about us. Out of the rain and into our kitchen stepped a police officer and the police chaplain. The chaplain's name is Barry Henson. He also serves as a pastor at the Life Center Church in Eatonville. He is a man I had known and respected in recent years, but that night I came to love him. He came delivering the worst news any parent could ever hear, and yet he did it with such care and sensitivity. I shall never forget what he said and what he did. Very gently, he said: "There has been a terrible automobile accident, and your son did not survive." He then told us what they knew of the circumstances. Then he embraced us in his great, strong, loving arms and prayed a deeply moving prayer. With his message, our hearts were shattered, but with his prayer, our broken hearts began the long, slow, still-continuing process of mending.

Because so many, many people have cared so deeply, and because I have been able to focus on little else in recent days, I would like to share with you some things I've learned all over again through the death of my son. Yes, I've learned all over again that life is uncertain, that we are just one step away from death. But I've also learned all over again that in the midst of life's uncertainty there are some things that last: faith, hope, and love.

I've learned all over again that, while life is uncertain, faith lasts.

It was the toughest thing I have ever had to do. I had to go down to the medical examiner's office to provide positive identification of my son. Thankfully, my friends, Dr. John Tolson and Dr. Buck Brown, went with me. As I looked at the lifeless face of my son, his eyelids now closed in death, I said: "It's over, but it's not over." Yes, his life on this earth was over. There was no denying that, and there was no denying the pain of that.

Our daughter, Meg Edington Sefton, whose love for her brother and whose love for language coalesced into some lines that poured out of her heart and rubbed up against my own feelings. Upon seeing her brother, his life now over, she wrote:

No life. I can't believe it. No blood pumping through all those tiny veins of your hand. I am in shock. No life. How can that be? When I looked at you there, it was as if all time had stopped, all time had come to a halt. All those molecules, all those atoms, all those neutrons, and electrons, and protons that are supposedly in constant motion, were not moving, for there was literally no minute, no second, no split second, no nanosecond. You did not breathe. You did not sit up. You did not open your eyes. I expected you to sit up. I expected you to look at us with your blue eyes and sly smile and shyly say something cute, or softly ask us, "What's wrong," or flippantly say, "I don't know what the big deal is; I'm just up here with God."

But there you lay, in the fine mahogany box. You're wearing a powder blue necktie and a plaid jacket. Your hair is parted over too far and swept to the side just a bit too neatly. Your face is waxy and your long fine nose seems more prominent than usual. Your hands are crossed just a bit too politely over your waist. I realize that the only time I would have seen you like this would have been in slumber. I realize that the only time I have seen you asleep was when you were a baby. It is only in dreams and in memories that I meet you now. I cry, but there is only the sound of my own echo.

I read your poetry and remember how I knew you. The thought that had crossed my mind when I first found out was that I would never speak with you again. I thought of this, and the breath was taken out of me. I could not find the breath and the silence crackled cold and hard, a sheet of ice across what is now an ocean of space. My mouth stands open, gaping, speechless, a silent red gash."

Meg's words capture the terrible pain all of us felt. John David's life was over. But my faith would not leave it there. My faith added the phrase . . . but it's not over. And there is no denying that, either. I shall see my son again.

It's over, but it's not over. I reflected on what I would have done in that circumstance if I had had no faith. If all I had been able to say was, "It's over," then I think I might have gone mad or tried to take my own life. And I wondered how anyone could ever face that kind of tragedy without faith. Being able to say, "It's over, but it's not over," turned unbearable grief into bearable sorrow.

Some years ago, the great Scottish preacher, Arthur John Gossip, lost his wife to tragic and untimely death. When he returned to his pulpit, he preached an incredibly powerful sermon that ended with these words:

I don't think we need to be afraid of life. Our hearts are very frail, and there are places where the road is very steep and very lonely. But we have a wonderful God. And as Paul puts it, what can separate us from his love? Not death, he says immediately, pushing that aside at once as the most obvious of all impossibilities. No, not death. For I, standing here in the roaring of the Jordan, cold to the heart with its dreadful chill and very conscious of the terror of its rushing, I can call back to you who, one day in your time, will have to cross it: Be of good cheer, my friend, for I feel the bottom and it is sound.[1]

That's the way I feel now. I don't preach from this pulpit a rose-colored glasses, health-and-wealth, pie-in-the-sky kind of faith. What I do here on Sunday morning is not some well-rehearsed, carefully scripted performance akin to the theatrical stage. I'm not up here to pander to my ego or to play word games with you. And don't dare try to tell me that I don't know what life in the real world is all about. Don't dare suggest that because I am a preacher I am somehow insulated and isolated from the real workings of our world. Dear friends, I have been to the bottom! I have been to where few of you ever have been or ever will be. I have been to where life hurts the most and cuts the deepest and hits the hardest. Therefore, listen to me when I tell you that faith in Jesus Christ is not some sideline pursuit, some pleasant diversion, some enjoyable hobby in your life. It's not something you give yourself to when it's convenient or when it helps you along your career track or when you want to appear respectable. It's not just a part of your life. You've got to see it as the center of your life, the foundation of your whole existence. Nothing else in your life really matters, nothing else in your life will last. When the police chaplain says, "Your son did not survive," I can tell you that you find out right then that the only thing you have left is faith. But because of my faith, I can say to you, "I feel the bottom, and it is sound." Faith lasts.

And I've learned all over again that while life is uncertain, hope lasts. William Sloane Coffin was, for a number of years, the minister of the Riverside Church in New York City. He and I come at the Christian faith from radically different theological perspectives, but we now share a common bond. In January of 1984, William Sloane Coffin's twenty-four year old son, Alex, lost control of his car on a rainy night in Boston, and plunged into the Boston Harbor. Alex died in the accident. Dr. Coffin said of his son, "He beat me at every game, and now, he has beaten me to the grave." What he then said made me realize that we not only have a common bond, but we also have a common hope. He said:

I know that when Alex beat me to the grave, the finish line was not Boston Harbor in the middle of the night. If a lamp went out, it was because for him, at last, the dawn had come.[2]

I think I would have said it differently. My son didn't beat me to the grave; he beat me to heaven! But while William Sloane Coffin and I may look at the faith from different perspectives, we do share the same hope. For my son, too, the dawn has come.

It was John Calvin, our Presbyterian ancestor, who said:

What would become of us if we did not take our stand upon hope, if we did not move through the darkness of this world on the path which is illumined by the word and the spirit of our God?

That's the hope on which I stand. And that hope was confirmed for me in a call I received from a young man named Robert Midden. I did not know him, but he called to let me know that he was following John David that night when the accident occurred. He told me that he immediately rushed over to the car, checked for a pulse, and found none. He said: "Your son died instantly." He then went on to say something that has simply confirmed the hope I hold so dear. He said: "I called the police, and then I waited until they arrived." He paused for a moment and then he spoke once more, "Dr. Edington, I am a Christian. I want you to know that I held your son and surrounded him with prayer until the police came." Do you have any idea what it means to me to know that when the dawn came for my son, there was a disciple of Jesus Christ there to pray him home? Yes, what would become of us if we did not take our stand upon hope? What would become of us indeed? Hope lasts.

And I've learned all over again that while life is uncertain, love lasts. I've known all along that life is serious and we dare not treat it lightly. I've known all along that we dare not put off until tomorrow what should be done today because tomorrow may never come. More times than I want to remember, I've stood at the graveside to bury the very young. I remember the time when the cemetery echoed with the sound of a twenty-one-gun salute and with heels clicking to attention as young soldiers handed the flag to a mother, who just days before, heard a representative from the Department of the Army say, "We regret to inform you that your son was killed in action near Khe Sanh." I remember the day when we carried out to the cemetery the body of a ten–year-old boy who had been struck by lightning in a terrible storm, and I don't know that I was ever able to answer his parents' question, why? I remember the time when I buried one of my best friends and his fourteen-year-old son. They were killed by a drunken driver, and I tried to preach and to pray as we placed them side by side in the cemetery, and I now know that I left a piece of my heart in that place. I remember just a few months ago Trisha and I flew to Texas to wrap our arms and hearts around a couple with whom we have shared life for twenty years, and I buried their son whose life had ended tragically after just twenty-four years. And, of course, I look back across my dozen years with you, remembering the young people in this congregation so bright and attractive and full of life, who have been cut down long before their time, and I've struggled for all I'm worth to try to help their families find a way to live on. Now, I, too have lost a son. That's why I go on to remember that God, our Father, had a son, and in great love, God gave that son to die for us. And God then sat by the grave of his only son and mourned awhile, until, on Easter, he gave to his son and to my son, and to all of us, life eternal. His love lasts.

Therefore, my friends, the great tragedy in life is not to die, not even to die young. The great tragedy is to die without having lived. And the ultimate tragedy is to die without having lived with Christ and for Christ.

Back when the five of us in the Edington family were in the Holy Land, one of the things that we did was to drive to the top of Mount Tabor, known as the Mount of Transfiguration, not far from Nazareth. The road to the top was terribly narrow and filled with treacherous curves. Our driver seemed determined for some reason, known only to him, to get us to the top in record time, and as a result, we went careening along this treacherous road, flirting with disaster the whole way. I was in the front seat, Trisha and the kids were in the back. Suddenly in the midst of this wild ride, John David leaned up and said, "Dad, let me have that little Bible you always carry in your pocket." I said, "Why?" He replied, "Because I think we're going to die on this mountain, and when I die I want to be reading the Bible so that God will know I belong to him." Needless to say, I handed him my Bible! We've always loved telling that story in our family. But, of course, God already knew that John David was his. You see, God so loved John David that he gave his only begotten son. The death of my son hurts. The wound is deep, but the wound is clean. For I know how I loved him, and how he loved me, and how God loves the both of us.

If you don't hear anything else in this sermon, please hear this; if you don't remember anything else from this worship service, please remember this; if you don't do anything else in response to this experience, please do this: love while you still can love. Make the most of any moments that are yours, because too soon they may be gone. Then you will be left with nothing but your memories. So build good memories in your life. I plead with you today, in the name of Jesus Christ, love—love those whom God has given you to love and love them while you still can. I did that. And now I am so glad. Love lasts.

I have been helped in recent days by recalling that in the year 1873, H. G. Spafford, a Christian lawyer from Chicago, placed his wife and four children on the ocean liner *Ville du Havre*, sailing from New York to France.[3] Spafford expected to join them three weeks later, after finishing up some business at home. The trip started beautifully, but on the evening of November 21, 1873, as the *Ville du Havre* plowed through the waters of the Atlantic, the ship was suddenly struck by another vessel, the *Lochearn*. Thirty minutes later, the *Ville du Havre* sank, with the loss of nearly all on board. Mrs. Spafford was rescued by the sailors of the *Lochearn*, but the four children were gone. Mrs. Spafford then wired a message to her husband. It read, "Saved alone." That night Spafford walked the floors of his rooms in anguish, but also in prayer. Toward morning, he told a friend named Major Whittle, "I'm glad to be able to trust my Lord when it costs me something." Several weeks later, Spafford sailed from New York to join his grieving wife on the other side of the Atlantic. As his ship crossed the precise spot in the ocean where the *Ville du Havre* had gone down, carrying his children to their death, he sat down and wrote a hymn. The words he wrote were eventually set to Phillip Bliss's tune, named for the ship on which his children died, *Ville du Havre*. The words he wrote have strengthened many a soul, and now they are strengthening mine.

When peace, like a river, attendeth my way,
When sorrows like sea billows roll;
Whatever my lot,
Thou hast taught me to say,
It is well, it is well with my soul.

Dear friends, it is costing me dearly to say this to you, but when the waters are deep in your life, when sorrows like sea billows roll, you can say, and know it will be true: In Christ, it is well, it is well with my soul. Amen.

NOTES

Foreword

1. An instructive account of the comeback of one congregation that lifts up the key variables is Randy Frazee, *The Come Back Congregation* (Nashville: Abingdon Press, 1995).

2. A brief but lucid statement on this question is Robert L. Randall, *What People Expect From Church* (Nashville: Abingdon Press, 1992).

3. For a longer discussion on the emergence of *interchurch cooperation* as an ideologically proper theme, see Lyle E. Schaller, *The Small Membership Church* (Nashville: Abingdon Press, 1994), pp. 59-77.

4. A study of 942 placements of congregational ministers in the 1655—1749 era revealed that the median length of a pastorate was approximately twenty-seven years. J. William T. Youngs, Jr., *God's Messengers* (Baltimore: Johns Hopkins University Press, 1976), p. 143.

5. A provocative, useful, and affirming discussion of identity or various "styles" of ministry is James O. Abrahamson, *Put Your Best Foot Forward* (Nashville: Abingdon Press, 1994). The author identifies and analyzes six different basic approaches to do ministry in today's world based on studies of twenty-five different congregations.

6. Ezra Earl Jones and Robert L. Wilson, *What's Ahead for Old First Church?* (New York: Harper & Row, 1974), pp. 67-75.

7. A wonderful description of an effective leader is offered by J. S. Minomiya, "Wagon Masters and Lesser Leaders," *Harvard Business Review*, March/April 1988.

8. For a discussion of this see Lyle E. Schaller, *The Seven-Day-a-Week Church* (Nashville: Abingdon Press, 1992).

9. Several approaches to off-campus ministries are described by Lyle E. Schaller in, *Innovations in Ministry* (Nashville: Abingdon Press, 1994), pp. 64-133.

10. For a longer discussion of this highly divisive issue, see Lyle E. Schaller, *The New Reformation* (Nashville: Abingdon Press, 1996), chapter 5.

NOTES

Introduction

1. Lyle E. Schaller, *Center City Churches* (Nashville: Abingdon Press, 1993), pp. 147-48.

1. Identity

1. *Christian Century*, March 10, 1993.
2. "Edington Ads Whet New Spiritual Appetite," *The Orlando Sentinel*, 12-16-90, p. 60.

2. Intention

1. Lyle E. Schaller, *Center City Churches*, p. 170.

3. Investment

1. Jim Wooten, "The Conciliator," *New York Times Magazine*, January 29, 1995, p. 28.

4. Initiative

1. Lyle E. Schaller, *Center City Churches*, p. 181.
2. Ibid., p. 148.

5. Integrity

1. Laurie Beth Jones, *Jesus, CEO* (New York: Hyperion, 1995), pp. 278, 279.
2. Lyle E. Schaller, *The Seven-Day-a-Week Church* (Nashville: Abingdon Press, 1992), p. 111.
3. Laurie Beth Jones, *Jesus, CEO*, p. 290.
4. Ibid., p. 217.

6. Involvement

1. Leonard Sweet, *FaithQuakes* (Nashville: Abingdon Press, 1994), p. 85.
2. Ibid., pp. 32-33.
3. Ibid., pp. 67-68.

7. Invitation

1. Leonard Sweet, *FaithQuakes*, p. 46.
2. Loren Mead, *The Once and Future Church* (New York City, The Alban Institute, 1991), pp. 16-18.

NOTES

8. Inspiration

1. Robert Kirkpatrick, *The Creative Delivery of Sermons* (New York: Macmillan, 1944), Foreword.

2. Leonard Sweet, *FaithQuakes*, p. 49.

3. Aubrey Brown, "Koinonia," *The Presbyterian Outlook*, July 17, 1995, p. 12.

4. John R. Claypool, *The Preaching Event* (Waco, Tex.: Word Books, 1980), pp. 86, 87.

5. John Leith, *An Introduction to the Reformed Tradition* (Atlanta: John Knox, 1977), p. 218.

Sermon: When the Waters Are Deep

1. Arthur John Gossip, "But When Life Tumbles In, What Then?" *The Protestant Pulpit*, compiled by Andrew Blackwood (Nashville: Abingdon Press, 1947), p. 204.

2. William Sloane Coffin, "Alex's Death," *A Chorus of Witnesses*, ed. Thomas G. Long and Cornelius Plantinga, Jr. (Grand Rapids: Eerdmans , 1994), p. 262.

3. Details in the last section of the sermon are drawn from *Our Jerusalem* by Bertha Spafford Vester (Garden City, N.Y.: Doubleday, Inc., 1950), pp. 23-46.